OLIVE & OLIVE OIL

The Mediterranean Diet

TRADITIONAL GREEK AND CYPRIOT RECIPES

EDITIONS
TOUBI'S

"Festivity in the wood," reconstruction of a Minoan wall painting by the painter Giorgis Angelinis, from the palace at Knossos, 1600-1500 BC.

© Copyright   MICHAEL TOUBIS PUBLICATIONS S.A.
                   Nisiza Karela, Koropi, Attiki.
                   Telephone: +30 210 6029974, Fax: +30 210 6646856
                   Web Site: http://www.toubis.gr

ISBN: 960-540-489-3

Olive oil is an integral part of the history, economy and culture of all the Mediterranean countries, especially Greece. For the Greeks, it is a way of life and an irreplaceable food throughout the centuries. Greeks are the greatest consumers of this wonderful "natural juice," and 70% of the fats they consume are derived from olive oil.

Today's urban lifestyle, resulting in population mobility, new forms of labour, new health conditions, etc., has raised the issue of the healthy diet in developed societies. This has meant that the quality and type of our nutrition have become increasingly important matters.

Science has contributed much to food technology in order to satisfy the continually increasingly demands of the population. But, these "technological" interventions are not always healthy. Olive oil is wonderfully nutritious, forming the basis for the renowned Mediterranean Diet. The Mediterranean Diet is a combination of foods that are perfectly balanced, guaranteeing long life, health and a positive psychological outlook. This book aims to provide consumers and all those interested with the right information to improve the quality of their diet, combining good health and vitality.

Contents

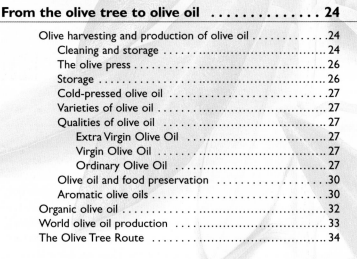

Recipes with olive oil

The olive: between myth and history

Mythology

Ancient Greek mythology relates that the goddess Athena, goddess of peace and wisdom, and the god of the sea Poseidon disagreed over who was to give their name to the new city of Attica.

Zeus, seeking to end their dispute, decided that the city would take the name of the god who offered the best gift to the residents of Attica. Poseidon threw his trident against a rock and cool water immediately gushed out from a spring. Athena hit the ground near the Erecthion temple on the Acropolis with her spear and an olive tree sprouted out. The olive tree was considered more valuable, since it could provide light, heat, food, medicines, cosmetics, etc. And so the city took the name of the goddess Athena. Tradition holds that this was the first Greek olive tree. The statue of Zeus Morios now stands at the point where Athena offered the first olive tree.

Another tradition says that Herakles brought the first wild olive tree to Greece from the banks of the river Danube and planted it at Olympia on his return. From Olympia, olive trees spread throughout the whole of Greece. The wreaths of the Olympic victors were made from the Olympian olive tree. The olive tree has always been a symbol of peace and reconciliation.

1. The Erectheion where, as Greek mythology tells us, the goddess Athena hit the ground with her spear and an olive tree sprung out.

2. Coin portraying the goddess Athena crowned with an olive wreath.

3. The goddess Athena alongside Kekrops, the mythical king of Athens, in front of the olive tree that she planted on the Acropolis rock.

The history of the olive tree

The so-called wild olive tree first appeared in the eastern Mediterranean region, and fossilised leaves that have been found have led scientists to believe that the history of the olive tree in this region dates back at least 60,000 years. The earliest written references to the production of olive oil have been found in Syria and Palestine, dating to the mid-3rd and the mid-2nd century BC respectively.

In Greece the use of olive oil was widespread in the Minoan and Mycenaean periods. Athletes throughout the whole of the ancient world would smother their bodies in olive oil before training and before and after competitions to keep themselves clean. We also know that the goddess Athena became the patron god of the city of Athens in the trial with Poseidon, because of her offer of an olive tree.

The olive tree was especially favoured in Egypt and Cyprus. In Egypt they would rub olive oil over the dead and dress them with necklaces made from twigs from the olive tree to guide them to their final abode. Cyprus, a leading olive oil producing country even today, always had excellent olive oil, light and good for the digestion, which the historian Strabo described as "euelaio," i.e. "exquisite olive oil."

During the Byzantine and Ottoman periods Greece had a high olive oil production, since the palaces of the nobles had an increased need for oil, for good food and lighting. However, when the Greeks began to rise up in 1821 the Turks, as punishment, burned many olive groves, condemning the Greek population to hunger and poverty.

Six thousand barrels of olive oil were exported from the port of Kalamata, one of the five main Greek ports, in 1800, indicating just how great olive oil exports were.

Today, olive oil cultivation continues to be highly developed in Mediterranean countries such as Greece and Cyprus. In many countries, including Greece, olive oil cultivation is protected by special legislation.

2

1. Detail from one of the Thera wall paintings, with the olive tree as an integral part of the subject matter. Xesti 3: "Refuse pit," North wall: detail from the wall painting of the "Worshippers."

2. These tablets found in north Syria and dating to the 3rd millennium BC are thought to be among the earliest written evidence for the cultivation of the olive tree.

3. Representation on a 5th-century BC red-figure kylix showing two athletes holding strigils and preparing to remove from their bodies the olive oil and sand that had gathered during their exercise. (Vatican Museum).

3

Minoan Art and the Olive Tree

Olive oil was widely used for religious purposes in Minoan Crete. The olive tree is a common motif in Minoan wall paintings, and this is because the olive tree was so widely grown that its artistic representation was a direct reference to Cretan flora in general.

Yet, there was also another, equally important reason as to why the olive tree appears so frequently in Minoan wall paintings. The Minoans recognised the beneficial qualities of olive oil, considering it to be such an important good that they made it a part of their religious rituals.

Many trees formed the focus of religious worship in the ancient world. At Knossos in particular the wall paintings which survive testify to the cultivation of the by now domesticated olive tree by the Minoans, and not simply the wild tree. This is indicated by the size of the leaves in the paintings.

The olive tree was a beloved theme of the Minoan wall painters: photo 1 shows the "Rhyton-carriers" and photo 2 the "olive tree grove," wall paintings from the palace at Knossos.

The Panathenaia

The Panathenaia, the ancient Athenians' most important festival, was held in honour of the city's patron goddess, Athena Pallas. Athletic contests were held during these great festivities. The victors of the games were awarded jars with olive oil as their prize, the so-called Panathenaic amphoras.

The Panathenaic amphoras were large, painted jars, 60-70 cm tall.

On one side was the goddess Athena wielding her shield and spear in battle stance, in between two columns. Until the 4th century BC there was a cockerel on her helmet, symbol of competition.

Alongside one column was the inscription "From the Games of the Athenians." This inscription was a guarantee of the origin of the jar and the quality of the olive oil. The sport in which the athlete had competed was depicted on the other side of the jar. From an inscription found on the Acropolis dating to 380 BC we learn of the number of jars which a winner and runner-up received.

The winner of competitions conducted in the nude (running, pentathlon, wrestling, boxing) would receive around 30 jars if he was a boy and 70 if he was an adult. The runner-up would receive around a fifth of the prize of a winner. In equestrian contests the winner would receive around 140 Panathenaic amphoras.

An average Panathenaic amphora would contain around 35-40 kilos of olive oil. The quantities of olive oil which the winners were awarded must have been very great.

The winner of the chariot race would take around 5 tons of oil. The athletes would use this oil for their own personal uses. They would smear their bodies with olive oil before training and competitions and they even used it to light their homes and for food. They would sell or export the rest of it.

The city of Athens required a total of 60-70 tons of oil for the victors. This oil would come from Athena's sacred olive trees, the Mories. The ancients believed that these olive trees stemmed from Athena's sacred tree on the Acropolis, the one that had sprouted when she hit her spear on the ground during the contest with Poseidon. The olive wreaths of the victors also came from these trees.

3. Pitcher-carriers from the representation of the Panathenaic parade on the Parthenon frieze, 447-432 BC, Athens, Acropolis Museum. The victors of the Panathenaic Games won trophies of amphorae filled with olive oil!

Kotinos, the Olympic Trophy

The olive tree was such an important good that it was honoured in many and interesting ways by the ancients. One of these was the crowning of Olympic victors with the kotinos, a wreath made from wild olive.

Let us take things from the beginning. The mythological founder of the Olympic Games was Herakles. One day, one of his brothers went to Olympia to participate in a road race, perhaps the first in history. Herakles had planted a wild olive tree nearby, which he had probably brought over from Crete, and crowned the victor with a wreath of twigs from the tree. Some time later Iphitos, on the advice of the Delphic oracle, established the kotinos as the trophy of the now official games staged at Olympia. There was even a tradition that the wild olive leaves be clipped with golden scissors by a young boy both of whose parents still lived. He would cut as many twigs as there were competitions and place them in the temple of the goddess Hera, on the gold and ivory table.

Plato's olive tree

A little beyond the Botanical Gardens in Athens, going towards the bridge of the Kifissos river, near the bank, stood until recently the so-called olive tree of Plato. It had been there for 25 centuries. The perimeter of the trunk is over 6 metres. The trunk has no bark and is full of holes, one of which is like a small cave. The Municipality of Athens, in order to protect it from the actions of wild animals and people, recently had it moved to the museum of the Agricultural University of Athens.

1. Coin portraying "Agon" (a divinity created by the Greeks as a personification of the competitive spirit). Here Agon is portrayed on a four-drachma coin from the island of Peparithos, winged and bearing two wreaths in his hands (London, British Museum).
2. The Olympic victor and his trainer represented with wild olive wreaths, proud to be the recipients of this great honour.
3. Vase with a representation of a victorious athlete. He holds olive tree wreaths and leaves, whilst woollen bands are wrapped around his arm and thigh (The Hermitage, St Petersburg).
4. Marble relief from Sounion showing a young man crowning himself (Athens Archaeological Museum).

In the Iliad, when Sarpedon is killed at Troy Zeus orders Apollo that he should be removed from the battlefield and olive oil be rubbed over his body. On this red-figure krater (ca 510 BC) in the Metropolitan Museum in New York we can see a representation of the removal of the dead Sarpedon. This is being done under the instruction of Hermes, however, and not of Apollo, as recorded in the Iliad.

Olive oil and religion

Olive oil plays a distinct role in the Christian Orthodox religion. It is a symbol of love and peace. It is a main component of the baptism ceremony, the Holy Chrism. Olive oil and flour are used during the ceremony of the Holy Unction. It is used to light church candelabra and the little lamp that lights the icon stands in village houses. Women used to make the sign of the cross over the ill using the oil from these lamps so that they would get well.

The ancient Greeks would smear olive oil over the bodies of the dead in order to protect them, and such scenes are depicted on many amphoras. In some villages even today they throw olive oil from the icon lamp over graves nine days after the burial.

There are many references to olive oil in the Holy Scriptures. When Noah sent the pigeon out from the ark it returned with the branch of an olive tree, this was a sign that God was no longer angry. In the Book of the Exodus, the Lord teaches Moses how to make an ointment using olive oil so that they could anoint the heads of the priests and kings during their consecration.

Olive oil has a special place for Orthodox Christians and is used in the baptism ritual (photo 1) as well as in the little candle in the icon stands (photo 2) and elsewhere.

The elixir of life and longevity

Evidence from Greece today demonstrates the true blessing of olive oil for the prevention of illnesses such as heart disease, diabetes, breast and prostate cancer. Olive oil makes a great contribution to a long life.

The olive oil of Greece is a natural juice and is one of the twelve most beneficial foodstuffs. If it is of high quality it is known as "extra virgin" and is one of the purest and healthiest fats consumed by man.

All types of oil, plant and animal, contain different kinds of fatty acids. These are divided into saturated, polyunsaturated and monounsaturated.

Olive oil contains only monounsaturated fatty acids as well as oleic acid, a major component of olive oil with a content of up to 80%. It gives health and long life and is superior to any other type of oil. It is an irreplaceable food.

The ancient doctor Hippocrates was the first to recognise the beneficial qualities of olive oil and he recommended it as a cure for many illnesses. Hippocrates believed that olive oil, wine and wheat constituted the basis of a good diet. The numerous health benefits of olive oil led Homer to describe it as the drink of the gods, the golden liquid.

All these and many other characteristics have led to the international recognition of Greek olive oil in the past few years.

In 1947 a group of scientists visited Crete. To their great surprise, despite the fact that the region was devastated after the war, the health of the residents was significantly better than that of Britons or Americans. The Cretans had an average of fewer deaths from cardiovascular diseases and cancer and they lived longer.

Extensive scientific research was first carried out in the 1950s in seven countries (Finland, the United States, Holland, Italy, Yugoslavia, Japan and Greece) to determine which countries had less deaths from cancer and heart disease, and which factors could help prevent such diseases. One thousand people aged between 40 and 59 from each country participated in the study. Over a period of 15 years, the researchers' attention was drawn to one region of the Mediterranean, to Crete. Not simply were there lower rates of deaths from cancer and heart disease on Crete, but life expectancy was also much higher.

Hippocrates, the father of medicine, and Homer, the great epic poet, early on realised the value of olive oil. In the photographs, the statue of Hippocrates at Kos (1) and the bust of Homer on Ios (2).

Finland, death rate from heart disease 97.2%
Holland 63.6%
Italy 46.2%
Yugoslavia 34%
Greece 20.2%
And for the region of Crete the rate was only 3.8%!

Whilst in the United States, the death rate from heart disease had already reached 77.3%.

Moreover, there were no deaths in Crete from cancer or other serious illnesses.

The researchers initially tried to explain the phenomenon in terms of the climate or the way of life of the residents of Crete. They soon came to the conclusion, however, that the long life of the Cretans was due to the significant quantity of olive oil that they consumed in comparison with other peoples, as well as the fruit and vegetables. On this island you meet happy old people!

The conclusions were that the Cretans age well because they eat well.

Recent reliable studies have also shown that among the peoples of the Mediterranean the Greeks have the most balanced diet. With basic ingredients of olive oil, fruit, vegetables, cereals, wine, fish, honey, and the wonderful herbs - produce with a high nutritious value - the Greek diet is a model for a healthy way of life, absolutely suited to the modern lifestyle.

Olive oil and medicine

Olive oil and cardiovascular diseases

Several studies conducted in the past fifteen years in both the European Union and the USA have confirmed the beneficial effects of olive oil for cardiovascular diseases. In the Greek regions of Crete and Mani in particular, where the diet includes aside from olive oil large quantities of vegetables, fruit, pulses, fish, etc., with little meat consumption, cardiovascular diseases are significantly reduced in comparison to those nations with a higher consumption of animal fats and meat.

It has been proved that olive oil reduces the level of low-density lipoproteins, i.e. "bad" cholesterol, and increases the level of high-density fatty proteins, i.e. "good" cholesterol. This reduces the deposition of fats on the walls of the arteries, reducing clotting of blood vessels and the heart.

More than any other natural produce, olive oil reduces cholesterol and so provides the heart with a wonderful protective shield.

Olive oil and ulcers

Olive oil does not upset the stomach, unlike animal fats. It reduces gastric fluids and helps treat ulcers. A spoonful of extra

virgin olive oil a day on an empty stomach helps the intestine to function properly and treats constipation.

Olive oil and skin
Olive oil contains vitamins A, B and E and protects human skin from the sun and burns.

Olive oil and the nervous system
Chlorophyll contributes to cell growth, and reinforces blood metabolism and strength. It plays a leading role in the development of the central nervous system. Olive oil is man's best source of energy

Olive oil and cancer
The therapeutic qualities against cancer (especially breast cancer) that the regular consumption of olive oil provides are well known. Harvard University Professor D. Trichopoulos calculates that the daily use of olive oil reduces the risk of breast cancer by around 25%.
It is not by chance that among the women of Crete and Mani, where olive oil is consumed in great qualities, breast and ovarian cancer are rare.

Olive oil and ageing
The antioxidant substances contained in olive oil help us to age well. Chlorophyll contributes to cell growth, and reinforces blood metabolism and strength. It plays a leading role in the development of the central nervous system.

Olive oil and bile
Helps bile thus aiding digestion.

Olive oil and bones
Olive oil contributes to a strong skeleton and bone growth. It is very important for the growth and composition of children's bones.
It plays a great role in the prevention of osteoporosis.

Olive oil and neuralgia
A massage with warm olive oil reduces pain.

Olive oil and the pancreas
It activates the pancreas to a significant degree so that diabetics often require less quantities of insulin.

Cosmetics

Olive oil is a natural source of beauty and life.

Since antiquity olive oil has been used for the manufacture of perfumes and cosmetics. During the Homeric era it was used exclusively for the care of the body. When he arrived shipwrecked on the island of the Phaeacians, Odysseus dusted himself down and then oiled his body with the olive oil given to him by the musical maids.

In the "Athenian Constitution," thought to have been written by Aristotle, it is mentioned that the victors of hippodrome races were awarded prizes of olive oil.

The ancient Greeks believed that olive oil made wrinkles disappear and delayed hair loss.

The athletes would smear their bodies with large amounts of olive oil before competing, as would warriors before a battle. The olive oil they used was of exceptional quality, and they would often fragrance it with herbs and aromatic plants. The process of cleaning was a ritual.

When there was no such thing as soap, olive oil played an important role in people's lives.

When a family could not produce or acquire its own olive oil, it became impossible to survive. The ancient Romans learnt to appreciate olive oil from the Greeks, for its uses as a cosmetic and to produce various types of essential oils.

Thanks to its protective fats, olive oil protects the skin from the harm caused by air pollution. It has revitalising, moisturising and softening qualities and for this reason is used in many moisturising creams, soaps and perfumes.

Moisturising face masks

1. Mix extra virgin olive oil with a little mud mask to create a smooth mixture. Apply to the face and leave for 5-10 minutes. Rinse with warm water.

2. Mix olive oil and water and beat as though preparing a mayonnaise. Apply to the face and leave for 10 minutes for deep moisturising.

For wrinkles

Prepare a mixture from olive oil and lemon juice and massage gently into your wrinkles before going to bed.

To soften the skin

Mix equal amounts of olive oil and salt. Massage over your whole body then rinse off.

For soft hands

1. Heat a little olive oil in a microwave oven and dip your hands in for ten minutes.
2. Mix one spoon of sugar with olive oil and massage over your hands for an amazing result.

For shiny, healthy hair

Mix the juice of one lemon with a little olive oil and an egg yolk. Lightly massage the mixture into your hair.

For dry hair

Mix some olive oil with a little rosemary and massage lightly into your hair for five minutes.

For tired feet

Lightly massage with olive oil and rosemary.

To strengthen the nails

Soak your fingers in warm olive oil for five minutes.

From the olive tree to olive oil

Olive harvesting and production of olive oil

The first step in the production of olive oil is the harvesting of the olives. The quality of the oil depends to an extent on the manner and time of harvesting. Olive cultivation is not difficult as the tree is tough and sturdy and the work is neither time-consuming nor laborious. The cultivation of the olive begins at the end of winter and lasts until the beginning of January. The best olive oil is to be got when the olive begins to change colour from green to black. At Olympia, in order to attain the best quality olive oil, they gather the olives as soon as they begin to change colour.

Soil and climatic conditions are two factors which influence the quality of the olive oil. Dry and rocky earth provides the best oil.

Harvesting is usually done by gathering the olives from the ground, having shaken or beaten the tree with a cane, or picking them directly from the tree by hand.

1. Ancient vase (520 BC) with a portrayal of olive gathering.

2. "The gathering of the olives," a work by the leading Greek popular painter Theophilos.

Picking by hand is the best way, as this does not "damage" or modify the fruit. In Mani, where the olive trees are small, gathering is done only from the tree. The oil produced from overripe olives taken from the ground does not have the best quality taste, fragrance or nutritional value.

Beating the tree with a cane does most damage to the tree and the fruit. The olives must be picked early enough so as to produce the best quality olive oil.

Cleaning and storage

Cleaning and storing of the olives follow on from the gathering. The olives are put into sacks or crates or directly poured onto the back of a truck and then taken to the olive press. The olive begins to deteriorate as soon as it is removed from the tree. This is the reason why they must be taken to the press as soon as possible, in order to produce the best quality olive oil.

The olive press

When the olives reach the press they are cleaned and any other matter, such as leaves, mud, sticks, etc., is removed. The olives are then put in the press where they are crushed and turned into pulp. The oil is got from the pulp either by squeezing or through centrifugal processes.

Storage

Storage is the last stage in the production of extra virgin olive oil. Attention must be paid so that the area in which the oil is stored is cool and dark (14 - 18 degrees Celsius). Olive oil's enemies include the sun, as it causes oxidisation and alteration of the oil. Olive oil is an exceptionally sensitive product. It is essential that we take especial care in storing it as it changes and absorbs smells from the surrounding environment. Today, when houses do not have enough room for storing olive oil in clay jars, a good place to keep it is in dark green bottles.

Fresh olive oil often appears "cloudy" because of small sediments that have remained. After a short while the body of the oil, the "mourga," settles at the bottom of the jar and creates an unpleasant aroma. For this reason, it is better to pour the olive oil into another jar after two months, to get rid of the mourga.

Around a month is required for production to be completed, for the qualities of the oil to mature, even if the taste of fresh olive oil is an absolute delight.

We should all be aware, however, that a good olive oil lasts for around 14-18 months. As they say in Greek, "old wine, new oil."

Cold-pressed olive oil

Cold-pressed olive oil is the most healthy as it is completely natural.

The olive press of Zavitsanos at Meganisi, Lefkada.

It is the first oil to come out of the classic old-style press, without the addition of warm water, which destroys its vitamins.

Over 5 kilos of olives are required to produce one kilo of cold-pressed oil.

Varieties of olive oil

The colour of an olive oil is an indication of its quality. The green oils are usually produced from unripe green olives. The colour varies in accordance with the provenance and the method of production, from deep green-yellow to gold. In contrast with what we used to believe, there is no particular taste that can be ascribed to olive oil.

In mild climates, where harvesting of the olives can be done throughout the whole of the winter until the early spring, the olive oil is sweet and fleshy. The new oil has a bitter and spicy taste.

In Greece, where olives are cultivated throughout the whole country, there are varieties to suit all tastes: sweet olive oil, fruity oil, spicy oil, oil with fragrant herbs, etc. Personal preference and the combination of foods are important criteria in the choice of olive oil.

Qualities of olive oil

The basic features of the quality of olive oil are acidity, oxidisation and colour.

The quality of an olive oil is not calculated solely by taste but also be acidity. In general, the lower the acidity the better the oil.

The level of acidity is determined by the International Olive Oil Council.

Extra Virgin Olive Oil

This is the highest quality olive oil. It is produced pure without high temperatures. Acidity does not exceed 1%. It has an exquisite aroma and colour. Perfect for salads and vegetables or with fresh bread or toast.

Virgin Olive Oil

Acidity does not exceed 1.5% - 2%. The aroma and taste are satisfactory. Suitable for frying and with "ladera" dishes (foods prepared in olive oil).

Ordinary Olive Oil

Acidity does not exceed 3%. Used mainly for cooking.

How to sample olive oil

The best way to sample the taste and quality of an olive oil is with bread. Bread has the quality of being able to neutralise the pit of the stomach and the taste of the olive oil can thus be fully sensed. The aroma of the oil allows us to determine its quality, type and production method precisely.

The choice of an oil is a matter of taste. What we should look out for is its quality as many low quality or adulterated olive oils are sold on the market.

A high quality olive oil is suitable for all uses.

Olive harvesting

Olive oil and food preservation

From long ago, when the methods we have today for preserving foods did not exist, people sought other ways to preserve their vegetables, meat, fish and cheese. One of the most natural ways was to preserve them in olive oil. In this way, food can be preserved for very long periods without losing n either its nutritional value nor its taste. It is well known that olive oil is a natural preservative, preventing air from coming into contact with the food and thus destroying it.

Basic principles of preservation:

The food must be completely dry. The jars that are to be used must also be completely clean and dry. Use extra virgin olive oil and cover the food completely. You must never, however, fill the jar right up to the top.

Aromatic olive oils

The decipherment of the Linear B tablets has given us much valuable information on the use of aromatic oils in religious rituals, as perfumes, in leather tanning and in the treatment of illnesses.

The gods of Olympus smeared their bodies with aromatic olive oils to make their muscles supple, their skin soft and for health purposes. Olive oil is a wonderful disinfectant. There are many valuable references in old Greek sources to recipes using aromatic olive oils. Some were used to add more taste to the oil or to bolster its antioxidant qualities. The most common aromatic plants and herbs are oregano, coriander, fennel, rosemary, bay leaves, thyme and basil. We can also add spices, garlic and chilli peppers.

Up until a few years ago it was still common for people to throw two sprigs of oregano into the olive oil jar to add taste.

Many aromatic olive oils are sold commercially, but we can also make them ourselves. They are used with salads and roast meats and with fresh and toasted bread.

A few drops of aromatic olive oil on your plate are enough to put you in a good mood!

A word of warning! Aromatic oils can be easily damaged, in particular when the bottle or jar is opened. It is therefore best to remove the herbs once the olive oil has absorbed their aroma. The aromatic plants must not be washed so that they do not lose their aroma; they must be perfectly dry. The jar which will be used must also be dry and sterilised.

Olive oil and fennel

In a bottle, add two glasses of extra virgin olive oil, 2-3 cloves and a sprig of fennel. Leave for two weeks in a cool, dark place.

Olive oil with basil

Pour two cups of extra virgin olive oil into a bottle or jar and add a couple of sprigs of fresh basil. If you wish, you can also add two cloves of garlic.

Store in a cool, dry place for two weeks.

Olive oil with chilli peppers

Pour two cups of extra virgin olive oil into a bottle or jar and add three whole chilli peppers. Store in a cool, dry place for one week.

Olive oil with garlic

Peel three cloves of garlic. Pour three cups of extra virgin olive oil into a bottle or jar. Add the garlic and seal tightly. If you wish, you can also add a little rosemary.

This aromatic oil adds an extra touch to salads and roast meats. It is natural, healthy and very tasty.

What can be more delicious than a slice of toasted bread with a drizzle of olive oil with garlic!

The few extra calories will recompense us with energy!

Olive oil with rosemary

Pour two cups of extra virgin olive oil into a bottle or jar and add a sprig of rosemary and two small peppers. Seal the bottle tightly.

Store in a cool, dry place for two weeks and then remove the rosemary and the peppers from the oil, so that it will last longer.

If combined properly, aromatic olive oils are a delightful treat for your palette.

Organic olive oil

The past twenty years have witnessed an effort to grow more organic foods, such as fruit, vegetables, wine, cereals, etc. Consumers believe that this produce is of a higher quality and nutritional value as no chemicals have been added.

Since 1993 Greece has been in line with European Union legislation on organic farming and the appropriate legal institutional framework for the development of organic farming is now in place.

In 1988 organic olive cultivation began in Mani and is spreading continuously.

According to recent calculations by the Ministry of Agriculture organic olive cultivation will soon reach 40,000 square kilometres. High quality organic olive oil is sold in dark glass bottles on which are mentioned the place of production as well as the number and inspection certification. (Warning: organic olive oil must bear the symbol of an approved certification agency).

Nutritional value of olive oil

Olive oil is a source of life, health and balance. It has a positive effect on all the stages of our growth from childhood until old age. It is a pure source of vitality with a great nutritional value. It forms the basis of the healthy Greek diet.

In relation to other vegetable and animal fats, olive oil:

- Has a lower level of triglyceride hydrolysis.

- Does not undergo much alteration when properly heated.

- Is absorbed in a satisfying way - almost the same as breast milk.

- Its oxide composition helps to avoid hyperoxide reactions and the appearance of free radicals which have a negative effect on the central nervous system and longevity.

World olive oil production

The International Olive Oil Council estimates that there are around 800 million olive trees in the world today. The area covered by these trees is greater than the state of Arizona in the USA and twice the size of England.

The greatest number of olive trees is to be found in the Mediterranean basin (around 98%). World olive oil production comes primarily from Spain, Italy, Greece, Portugal, Tunisia, Algeria and Morocco.

Spain is considered the largest olive oil producer in the world. Then follows Italy, Greece, Tunisia, Turkey, Syria, Morocco, Israel, Portugal, Algeria, Jordan, Palestine, Argentina, Libya, France, Cyprus etc.

Olive trees are cultivated throughout almost the whole of Greece: the Peloponnese, Central Greece, Thessaly, Epirus, Macedonia, Thrace, the Aegean islands (with Lesbos as the centre), Crete, the Ionian islands and the Dodecanese.

Thera are around 120 million olive trees in Greece, producing the best olive oil in the world! There are also 3,000 olive presses in operation, whilst 450,000 families make their living from the olive tree and its products.

Greeks are the world's biggest consumers of olive oil.

The town of Kalamata in the southern Peloponnese is especially famed, both for its olives and its olive oil.

ANNUAL OLIVE OIL PRODUCTION

Olive oil production in tones	0	100	200	300	400	500	600	700	800
Spain									701
Italy						500			
Greece					360				
Tunisia			169						
Turkey		102							
Syria	91								
Morocco	51								
Israel	47								
Portugal	38								
Algeria	33								
Jordan	14								
Palestine	9								
Argentina	8								
Libya	7								
France	3								
Cyprus	2.5								
Iran	2								
Croatia	1.6								
USA	1.2								
Egypt	1.1								
Australia	0.7								

The world's leading olive oil producing countries and their average annual oil production (average for the period 1990-2000), details provided by the IOOC.

The Olive Tree Route

The olive tree has been a symbol of peace, fertility, purity and well being for thousands of years. Today it continues to unite nations and to send a message of hope and peace to all those who follow its trails.

The Olive Tree Route aims to organise and institutionalise a series of cultural and other events which have the olive tree and its products as their focus. The primary goal is the international promotion of the olive tree, its role in the economy and the value of its products for people.

The concept for the Olive Tree Route came from the Messenia Chamber of Commerce.

A specially designed trail for motorcyclists begins each year at ancient Pylos, ending at that year's Mediterranean Cultural Capital. It passes through olive-producing regions, archaeological sites, Mediterranean cities and regions filled with olive trees. Many cultural events take place during the trail and when it terminates at the Cultural Capital.

The aims of the Trail are to link the culture of the olive with tourism, the creation of an international network of activities, the direct collaboration and exchange of experience between businesses, producers, co-operative organisations and local government, as well as for Greek and foreign consumers to meet.

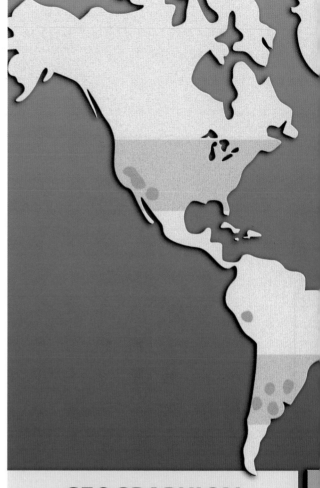

GEOGRAPHICAL DISTRIBUTION OF OLIVE TREE CULTIVATION

 Boundaries of olive cultivation

 Olive oil producing zones

 **Zones of extensive cultivation**

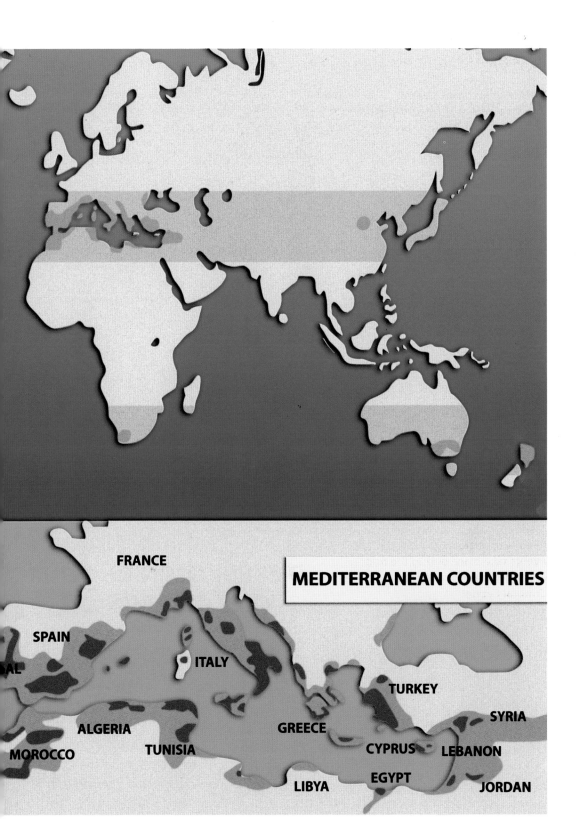

FRANCE

MEDITERRANEAN COUNTRIES

SPAIN

AL

ITALY

TURKEY

SYRIA

ALGERIA

GREECE

MOROCCO

TUNISIA

CYPRUS

LEBANON

EGYPT

LIBYA

JORDAN

Twelve reasons for saying «yes»!
to Greek olive oil

- The roots of the olive tree are deeply embedded
in the soil and the history of the country

—❧❦—

-The wisdom of experience in olive cultivation is combined
with scientific research.

—❧❦—

-The climatic conditions and ecosystem are favorable
to the cultivation of the olive tree.

—❧❦—

-The type of olive grove is a determining factor in the fruit-bearing cycle.

—❧❦—

-Enthusiasm for the olive grove is linked to the knowledge
and experience of Greek olive-growers.

—❧❦—

-The most suitable varieties are always selected for any given bootie.

—❧❦—

-The most appropriate harvesting techniques are used and the degree of ripeness
of the fruit is always taken into account.

—❧❦—

-Suitable measures are taken to clean the fruit before
it is sent for processing.

—❧❦—

-The length of time the fruit is stored before pressing ensures
that the product has a long life.

—❧❦—

-The correct methods of olive-pressing are used.

—❧❦—

-Standardization and storage are carried out in the right conditions
to ensure consistent quality

—❧❦—

-Quality control is carried out on the final product, the olive oil,
and it is checked for its wholesomeness.

The olive tree reigns. It emerges suddenly
from the silver ash and gives life its new
shade. The paths in the fields are filled
with voices, with the noble foliage.
This is the boundless forest that fills the
island. Millions of trees unfold their
blessing from one end to the other, over the
mountains, the valleys, down to the beach.
They clamber up to the highest peaks, tumble
down the gales, bend over the waves and hang
on to the cracks in the rocks.
Wherever there is a handful of earth, a root
has been laid down. Wherever God didn't
put even this handful of earth, the peasants
carry it on their backs, in the wicker baskets.
They build a little terrace where the earth
is soft, build a dry stone wall and plant a
new olive tree there. All the mountains are
engraved with these steps. "Feet steps"
the locals call them, using the word
of the ancient ancestors. Over these steps
the sacred trees tread, clambering up to the
highest peaks. Generations and generations
lived and died lovingly bent over this here
earth, bearing fruit with it like a woman.
Through such a struggle was the infinite forest
resurrected over the great island, so much toil
is covered by the branches of peace
and silence. And now its leaves flutter
summer and winter next to the fir tree,
whilst in the spring it wears the budding
pomegranates and the other fruit trees like
an ornament..

Stratis Myrivilis

Olive Varieties

It has been estimated that there are around 600 varieties of olives in the world, although there is some doubt as to their classification and description.

The varieties have been differentiated on the basis of the characteristics of the trees and their leaves, in particular the fruit and the stone. It is acknowledged that the features and the produce of a variety are influenced by the climate and territory of the area where they are cultivated. From this perspective, the characteristics of the stone are more sound. In any case, each variety is made up of many different individual olives, and it is very common for differences to be observed between olives of the same variety. This adds to the confusion surrounding the classification of olives. It has been suggested that basic distinctions between the varieties could be identified through the methods by which they are processed, although this has not yet completely solved the problem.

In Greece the problem is exacerbated by the various local names that are given to each variety. The same name can be used for several different varieties, whilst one variety can be grown under different names in different regions.

It is believed that around 40 different varieties are grown in Greece today, which can be classified as:

- table or edible olives
- oil-producing olives
- double, or mixed, usage.

For table olives, the fruit must be large, the ratio between flesh and stone be as high as possible, the oil content low, the skin fine, whilst the flesh should be solid and come away from the stone easily. A high sugar content is an asset, helping to preserve the olive.

Oil-producing olives should have a higher oil content, be as large as possible, and the quality of the oil (aroma, taste, etc.) be satisfactory.

Below we give a short presentation of the best olive varieties grown in Greece, whilst the table indicates other names by which they are known and the main regions in which they are grown.

THE MOST IMPORTANT OLIVE VARIETIES IN GREECE		
VARIETY	OTHER NAMES	MAIN REGIONS
TABLE OLIVES		
Conservolea	Amfissis, Artas, Violiotiki, Hondrolia Halkidikes	Central and W. Greece, Halkidike
Kalamata	Kalamatiani, Aetonychia, Korakolia	Peloponnese, Crete, W. Greece
OIL-PRODUCING OLIVES		
Koroneiki	Lianolia, Psilolia, Ladolia, Kritikia	Peloponnese, Crete, Ionian Islands
Lianolia Kerkyras (Corfu)	Souvlolia, Korfolia, Prevezana, Dafnofylli	Corfu, Paxi, Cephalonia, Zakynthos, Epirus coast
Koutsourelia	Patrini, Patrinia, Lianolia, Ladola	Peloponnese, Nafpaktos
Mastoedes	Tsounati, Matsolia, Mouratolia	Peloponnese, Crete
DOUBLE USE		
Megareitiki	Perachoritiki, Vovoditiki, Hondrolia Aiginas	Attica, Boeotia, Kynouria
Kolovi	Mytilinia, Valanolia	Lesbos, Chios
Kothreiki	Manaki, Manakolia, Korinthiaki	Delphi, Amfissa, Troezen, Kynouria
Thrubolea	Thasitiki, Hondrolia Evoias	Aegean islands, Attica, Euboea

Table Varieties

Conservolea

This is the most common table olive, especially the green variety. This is a very productive variety when cultivated on good soil and irrigated, with a relatively good tolerance to the cold. It ripens relatively early (November), and there is much variation, with many different local names (Amfissis, Artas, Violiotiki, etc.). The Hondrolia Halkidikes is believed to belong to this variety. The Conservolea tree grows to a great height, with long, average-size leaves that have a distinctive tip at the end, with a downward bend.

The fruit is large, oval, with a dark, chewy flesh that comes away from the stone easily. The fruit weighs 5.5 - 8.0 grams. It is harvested when green to produce the green table olive or, more rarely, when black for black olives.

Kalamata or Kalamon

This is the best variety for the production of select (seasoned in brine) table olives. It requires moisture, is of average but stable productivity, and the fruit ripens fairly early (late November-December).

It is characterised by a tree of average height with broad, deep green leaves. The fruit is elongated with a narrow stone that comes away from the flesh easily. The fruit weighs 5-6 grams, has a flesh : stone ratio of 8-10 to 1, and an oil content of around 20%.

Oil-Producing Varieties

Koroneiki

This is the leading Greek oil-producing variety, with a great productivity and excellent quality oil. It is adaptable to dry and moist regions, with a yield of 30-100 kilograms of fruit per tree, depending on the conditions. It has a very high yield in adverse conditions, whilst with irrigation it yields less.

This variety ripens early (beginning in early October) with few demands during the winter cold for bearing fruit.

It is characterised by its small leaves and large fruit. The fruit is spherical in shape with one curved side. It weighs around 1 gram and has dimensions of 12-15 x 7-9 mm. It has an oil content of 15-27%, which is considered very good. The stone has the same shape as the fruit, and also has a curve on one side, ending in a peaked tip. The flesh : stone ratio is 5 to 1.

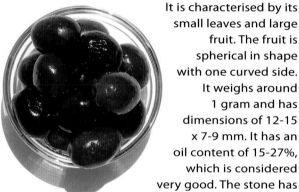

Black large Volos olives.

Lianolia Kerkyras

Another important oil producing variety, producing excellent quality oil. It flourishes even on barren, stony ground although has greater demand for moisture (being cultivated primarily in areas with a large rainfall).

This variety has a lively vegetation and the trees can be very large. It is a late-ripening variety and its fruits are harvested late, after the first spring months. This late ripening encourages a high yield.

The large leaves that fold over upwards are characteristic of this variety, whilst the fruit is small, elongated, with a slight tip at the top. It weighs 1.1 - 1.8 grams, with dimensions of 18 x 7 mm and an oil content of around 20%. The stone is relatively large, elongated, with a tip at both ends. The flesh : stone ratio is 3-4 to 1.

Koutsourelia

This variety has an average productivity that prefers rich or average composition soil. It does not grow well at great heights. The fruit is rich with a good quality oil, ripening relatively early (from the end of October).

The tree is of average size with short shoots. The leaves are small. The fruit is round and ends in a small, lightly curved tip. The stone is relatively small with a tip at both ends. It weighs around 1.2 grams, with dimensions of 16.5 x 10 mm and an oil content of around 24-30%.

Mastoedes

This variety is spherical in shape, (mastoedes means breast shaped) then, with an average to low yield with a demand for good soil (deep, lime content). It blossoms late and can be cultivated at great heights (up to 1,000 m).

This variety ripens late (late December - early January).

The leaves are of average size with a prominent central fibre on the upper surface ending in a pronounced tip.

The fruit is of average size (2-2.8 grams), with the shape of a lemon and a large tip. The flesh : stone ratio is 6-8 to 1, and the oil content 20-30%.

Double Use Varieties

Megareitiki

This variety has a low demand for moisture and can be cultivated in dry areas (Attica) and also a low demand during winter cold for blossoming. Its productivity is considered to be average and it is not high-yielding, unless it is well tended.

It ripens relatively early (November - December). It has large leaves (10 x 75 mm) which end in a pronounced tip. The fruit varies. The typical shape is conical, with a narrower base and a peak at the tip. The fruit has an average weight of 4.2 grams, and the flesh : stone ratio is 6.5-7.5 to 1.

The fruit is double use, for olive oil and various average-quality table olives (mainly tsakistes).

Kolovi

This is the dominant variety in Lesbos. It has average demands for soil and tending, and in favourable conditions it can reach high yields. It is considered to be one of the best oil-producing varieties, both in terms of productivity and quality.

This variety ripens late (full ripening in February-March), although harvesting starts early (November).

The leaves are large, tough and relatively broad. The fruit is characterised by the absence of a teat or tip and it has an oval or spherical shape.

It is, however, usually narrower at the base and broader at the top (it looks like an oak seed). The fruit has a weight of 3-4.5 grams, oil content of 25-30% and a flesh : stone ratio of 2.5-5 to 1.

Kothreiki

A variety tolerant to dry conditions, cold and strong winds, flourishing to a height of up to 750 metres. Its yield is considered to be average, with average soil and tending demands.

The fruit is spherical without a teat, weighing 4-4.5 grams. The flesh : stone ratio is 3.5-7 to 1 and the oil content around 25%.

It is double use and a significant portion of the annual yield is used in the processing of table olives for the production of large or average-size salted black olives, which are of excellent quality, delicious and with a good aroma.

Green olives stuffed with red pepper.

Thrubolea

Produces an average-size fruit, weighing 2.5-5 grams, with a flesh : stone ratio of 5-7 to 1. It is double use with an oil content of up to 30%. The edible olives ripen on the tree, and are known as thrubes. The fruit requires high moistures and a relatively high temperature in the autumn, whilst the action of fungi leads to natural fermentation, meaning that the olives lose their bitter taste whilst still on the tree. Once they have dropped naturally to the floor, they are harvested, cleaned and preserved in brine.

Dried Amfissis olives.

The details above come from the magazine "Farming and livestock rearing," issue 3, page 12, March 2001

Edible Olives

The fruit of the olive cannot be eaten direct from the tree. The various substances in the skin give it a bitter taste, and it is necessary to process the olives to make them edible. This involves soaking out their bitterness and can be done in several ways. Specifically:

A. Store the olives in a jar with water and 10% salt for around six months. Then make a small slice in them with a knife and soak them in water again. Change the water every other day for twenty days. After twenty days taste the olives; if they do not taste bitter then they are ready.
Salt them and soak them in vinegar for a few hours.
B. The olives can also be stored dry with salt to remove the bitter flavour. When these olives are ready they will be all wrinkled.
C. Alternately soak and rinse the olives for several months.
D. Leave the olives to soak in olive oil for several months.
E. Store the olives in a strong alkaline solution for several days.

Once the bitter taste has been removed from the olives following one of the above methods, salt them and store them in olive oil. You can also add thyme or dried orange peel or some other aromatic herb to the oil, giving the olives a delicious flavour.

Green olives in vinegar
- 5 kilos large green olives
- 5 kilos water
- 1/2 kilo salt
- 2 kilos vinegar
- 1 1/2 kilos olive oil
- 2 kilos water
- 200 grams salt

Make a small slice in the olives on one side and put them in a large bowl with water. Leave for twenty days, changing the water each day. Prepare a solution with the 5 kilos of water and 1/2 kilo of salt and leave the olives in this brine for 10 days.
Throw this brine away and prepare another with the 2 kilos of water and the 200 grams of salt.
Add the vinegar and store the olives in this solution. They will be ready in three days.

Salted olives
- 5 kilos good quality green-black olives
- 5 kilos water
- 250 grams salt
- 150 grams sugar

Wash the olives and put them in a large clay or glass container. Prepare a brine, i.e. a solution of the salt diluted with water, and pour it over the olives. Every second day (for two weeks) change the water with the same brine. The last time that you change the water, add 150 grams salt and 50 grams sugar to the brine.
Leave the olives in the brine for two months before beginning to consume them.

The Mediterranean Diet

The Mediterranean Diet is a model for a healthy life

After a whole series of studies, scientists have come to the conclusion that the Mediterranean peoples have a longer life expectancy than other peoples - especially the people of Crete. It has been observed that Greeks consume less butter and more olive oil than any other European Union nation.

The Mediterranean Diet does indeed contain produce that is rich in antioxidants and "good" cholesterol. The Mediterranean Diet is based on bread, fresh fruit and vegetables, fish, olive oil, garlic, onions, herbs and fragrant wild greens.

Traditional Mediterranean Diet

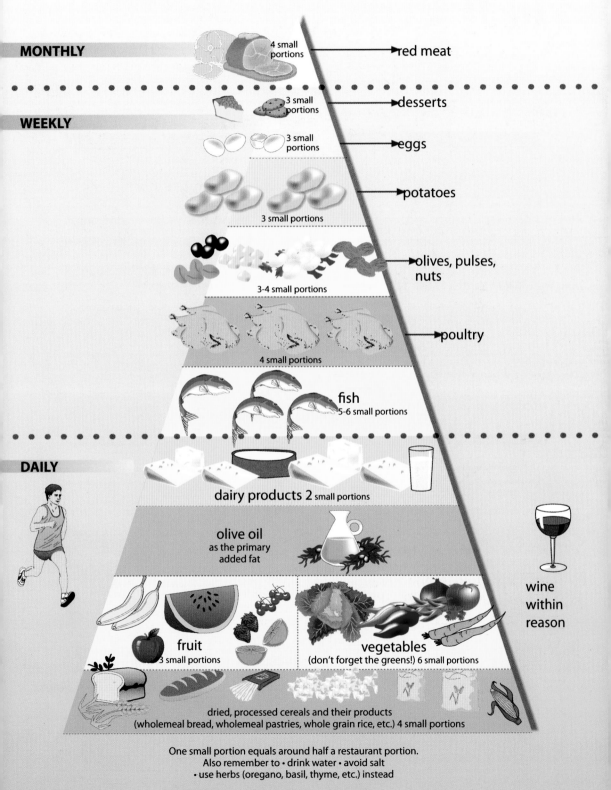

MONTHLY

4 small portions → red meat

WEEKLY

3 small portions → desserts

3 small portions → eggs

→ potatoes
3 small portions

→ olives, pulses, nuts
3-4 small portions

→ poultry
4 small portions

fish
5-6 small portions

DAILY

dairy products 2 small portions

olive oil
as the primary
added fat

wine
within
reason

fruit
3 small portions

vegetables
(don't forget the greens!) 6 small portions

dried, processed cereals and their products
(wholemeal bread, wholemeal pastries, whole grain rice, etc.) 4 small portions

One small portion equals around half a restaurant portion.
Also remember to • drink water • avoid salt
• use herbs (oregano, basil, thyme, etc.) instead

www.paidiatros.gr/51/index.html

Olive oil was used for cooking from a very early stage. In the era after the Homeric poems, Aristophanes, in his play the "Thesmophoriazusai," mentions olive oil, wine and flour as being essential to the daily diet.

One of the beloved foods of the ancient Greeks was "myttopos," a type of garlic dip made with cheese, honey, garlic and olive oil. From Aristophanes we also learn of "fries," a snack made of flour and oil cooked in olive oil and sold in the streets.

Much has changed from Aristophanes' times until today. Yet, olive oil still remains a basic ingredient of many delicious foods. The pages that follow contain many traditional Greek and Cypriot recipes.

Try them and see for yourself!

Traditional greek and cypriot recipes for:

- Salads
- Sauces
- Appetisers
- Ladera
  (dishes cooked in olive oil)
- Pulses
- Meat dishes
- Fish and Sea-food
- Desserts

Salads

Salads can be divided into two categories: cooked and raw. Cooked salads include the various wild greens and vegetables, such as radishes, courgettes, beetroot, string beans and artichokes. These are eaten with pure virgin olive oil and lemon or vinegar. Raw salads are a matter of creativity and imagination. A great salad can be made from the various seasonal vegetables to be found at the greengrocers. Grate some white and red cabbage, chop a little lettuce, carrots, spring onions, dill and parsley, slice a leek, add a little uncooked spinach, rocket, peppers of any colour and whatever else comes to mind. Mix together, add salt, black pepper, tomatoes, cucumber and pure virgin olive oil.

GREEK SALAD

- *3 red tomatoes*
- *1/2 cucumber*
- *1 onion*
- *1 green pepper*
- *black olives*
- *feta cheese*
- *capers • oregano • salt • vinegar*
- *1/2 tea cup olive oil*

Chop the tomatoes and onions
and slice the onion and pepper.
Place in a salad bowl and add
the capers, oregano, salt,
and feta cheese in small pieces.
Pour over the olive oil
and vinegar.

MACEDONIAN TYROKAFTERI
(SPICY CHEESE DIP)

- *1/4 kilo soft feta cheese*
- *1 hot green pepper*
- *4-5 soup spoons olive oil*
- *a little vinegar*

Grill the pepper, remove the skin
and seeds and chop into small pieces.
In a bowl, crush the cheese with
a fork. Add the olive oil, vinegar
and pepper and mix well until smooth.
This dish goes well with fried potato
chips and fried courgettes.

BLACK-EYE BEAN SALAD

- *1/2 kilo black-eye beans*
- *1/2 tea cup parsley, finely chopped*
- *4 soup spoons extra virgin olive oil*
- *1/2 cup spring onions, finely chopped*
- *oregano*
- *olives*
- *capers*
- *vinegar*

Cook the beans in plenty of salted water. Drain and place in a bowl. Add the rest of the ingredients and pour over the olive oil and vinegar. A tasty and healthy salad that makes your heart beat soundly!

CAULIFLOWER SALAD

- *1 cauliflower (2 kilos)*
- *1/2 cup of olive oil*
- *2-3 lemons*
- *salt*

Clean the cauliflower and remove the stem, then re-wash well. Bring a pan of water to the boil, adding salt, then put the cauliflower in. Boil for 25 minutes approximately.
Drain and serve warm with oil and lemon juice.

TZATZIKI

- *2 medium-sized cucumbers*
- *1 1/2 cups of yoghurt (strained)*
- *4-6 cloves of • garlic crushed*
- *a little vinegar • salt*

Skin the cucumbers and cut into thin strips with a vegetable grater; and then chop into small pieces. Drain and squeeze well and then salt. Add the crushed garlic, the vinegar, the yoghurt and mix, finally adding the oil. If you wish, you can sprinkle the tzatziki with paprika and garnish with olives.

POTATO SALAD

- *1 kilo potatoes • 3 small hard tomatoes chopped into small pieces*
- *1/2 cup olive oil*
- *Olives • capers*
- *gherkins*
- *parsley • vinegar*
- *salt*
- *black pepper*
- *3 spring onions, finely chopped*

Boil the potatoes and chop them into small cubes. Put them in a salad dish. Add the tomatoes, onions, capers, finely chopped parsley, salt and pepper. Drizzle with olive oil and vinegar. Sprinkle oregano over the top.

BEETROOT SALAD

- *1 kilo of beetroot*
- *oil and vinegar*
- *salt*

Clean and wash the beetroots.
Remove the stems and
the leaves. Boil the beetroots
for 20 minutes, then add the
leaves and boil for a further
half hour. After this, strain
them. Remove the outer skins
from the beetroots while
they are still hot, then cut into
slices. Serve with oil
and vinegar, or if preferred,
with a garlic dip.

KYTHNOS MELITZANOSALATA (AUBERGINE DIP)

- *3 large aubergines*
- *1/2 cup extra virgin olive oil*
- *2 cloves garlic, crushed*
- *vinegar • parsley and salt*
- *hot pepper (optional)*

Cook the aubergines whole in an oven
or barbecue until they have softened.
As soon as they have cooked run them
under a cold tap so that the skin can be
removed easily. Chop into small pieces
(do not put them in the liquidiser). In
a bowl, mix the aubergines, olive oil,
vinegar, finely chopped parsley and
garlic. You can add a finely chopped
tomato if you wish. A wonderful
summer mezze dish, to be accompanied
with a little ouzo on the beach.

Sauces

Sauces are another, often necessary, addition to food. Although sauces may not be Greek in inspiration or origin, they have been successfully "imported" into many Greek recipes, enriching their flavour. Attention is needed, however, in both their preparation and combination, as the wrong choice can literally render the most delicious Greek dishes useless.

Remember: more is not always best.

OLIVE OIL AND LEMON SAUCE

- *1 cup extra virgin olive oil*
- *1/2 cup lemon juice*
- *a little salt*
- *oregano or thyme*

Thoroughly whisk all the ingredients together. Pour over grilled fish and lobster cooked over charcoal, sprinkle with oregano or thyme.

GARLIC SAUSE

- *4 cloves of garlic*
- *1 cup of olive oil*
- *3 heaped tablespoons of flour*
- *vinegar* *salt*

Put some of the flour in a saucepan to brown. Crush the garlic and the salt together and add the vinegar. Stir this in the saucepan, pouring in some water. As soon as it boils and thickens a little, the sauce is ready to be used.

TOMATO SAUCE

- *1 kilo ripe tomatoes*
- *1/2 cup olive oil*
- *2 onions*
- *1 clove garlic*
- *salt and black pepper*
- *basil*

Slice the onions and the tomatoes. Heat the olive oil in a saucepan and fry the onions and garlic for about five minutes until browned. Add the tomatoes and stir using a wooden spoon. Add 2 glasses water, salt and pepper and heat slowly for half an hour, until the sauce thickens. Garnish with basil, as an accompaniment to pasta dishes.

HOME-MADE MAYONNAISE

- *2 egg yolks*
- *2 tea cups extra virgin olive oil*
- *white pepper* *salt*
- *juice of half a lemon*
- *3 soup spoons vinegar*

In a bowl, use a wooden spoon to beat the egg yolks with some of the olive oil. When the mixture begins to stiffen, add the remaining olive oil drop by drop. When the mayonnaise has solidified, mix in the pepper, salt, vinegar and lemon juice.

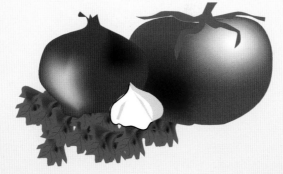

Appetisers

By appetisers, we mean
the various tasty side dishes
that can accompany a glass of ouzo
or an aperitif.
Delicious sun-dried tomatoes,
bulbs, fried olives, pickles, pies,
courgette balls and many more
tasty recipes. Bon apetit!

SUN-DRIED TOMATOES WITH OLIVE OIL

• *1 kilo tomatoes* • *2 cups olive oil* • *salt*

Choose ripe tomatoes. Clean well and dry. Cut in half
and place the tomato halves side-by-side on a baking tray.
Sprinkle with salt and leave in the sun for four days.
Put the sun-dried tomatoes in a jar and cover with olive oil.
Add two cups of lemon. Keep in the fridge.

BULBS

• *1 kilo bulbs*
• *3-4 cloves garlic*
• *1 cup olive oil*
• *2 cups vinegar*

Peel the bulbs in the same
way as onions and boil
them for half an hour,
changing the water
2-3 times so as to
remove the bitter taste.
Remove, leave to cool
then place in a jar. Add
one cup olive oil and two
cups vinegar. Keep in
the fridge.

PICKLE

- *300 grams courgettes*
- *200 grams carrots*
- *3-4 pieces of cauliflower*
- *2-3 long green peppers*
- *celery*
- *2 spoons black pepper*
- *1 spoon salt*
- *2 cloves garlic*
- *1 sliced onion*
- *1 stick cinnamon*
- *3 cups vinegar • 3 cups water*
- *1 cup olive oil*

Clean all the vegetables well and cut into chunks. In a saucepan boil all the vegetables with the salt, pepper and cinnamon for ten minutes. Drain and leave the vegetables to cool. Place them in a jar. Pour over the vinegar, olive oil and add more salt. Seal the jar well. Do not fill the jar right to the top.

FRIED OLIVES

- *1 cup de-seeded black olives*
- *4 soup spoons olive oil*
- *1 onion*
- *1 soup spoon oregano*
- *1 cup wine or vinegar and black pepper*

Finely chop the onion and fry in a pan with a little water, until the onion has softened and absorbed the water. Add the olives and oregano and stir. Mix and gradually add the wine or vinegar and pepper. Serve with chilled ouzo.

PICKLED AUBERGINES AND PEPPERS IN OLIVE OIL

- *3 small aubergines, sliced*
- *2 lemons, peeled and sliced*
- *3 soup spoons salt*
- *3 red peppers, sliced*
- *1 cup extra virgin olive oil*

Boil the aubergine slices for ten minutes. Drain and dry on kitchen paper. In a jar, place alternate layers of aubergine, peppers, and lemon slices (aubergine, peppers, lemon, aubergine, etc.). Sprinkle with salt and cover with olive oil. Seal the jar tightly.

KOLOKYTHOKEFTEDES (COURGETTE BALLS)

- *1 kilo courgettes, grated*
- *2 large onions, grated*
- *mint, finely chopped*
- *4 eggs*
- *1/2 kilo feta cheese, grated*
- *200 grams hard cheese, grated*
- *black pepper*
- *flour*

Mix all the ingredients well in a large bowl until the mixture has thickened. Shape into balls. Heat the oil in a frying pan and add the balls with a soup spoon. Fry at a medium heat until they are browned. Leave them on kitchen paper for the oil to dry out and serve at once.

SPANAKOPITTA (SPINACH PIE)

- *1 kilo spinach*
- *2 sheets fyllo pastry*
- *dill*
- *2 eggs*
- *salt and pepper*
- *2 spring onions*
- *2-3 leeks*
- *250 grams feta cheese*
- *1 cup olive oil*

Clean the spinach well.
Finely chop the spinach, leeks, dill and onions and squeeze with your hands until all their liquid is strained.
Add the feta cheese and eggs and mix.
Oil a baking tray with olive oil and lay down a sheet of fyllo pastry.
Spread the mixture over the pastry.
Cover with the other sheet of fyllo pastry and drizzle olive oil over the top.
Slice the pie into portions and cook in a pre-heated oven at 180 degrees for 1 1/2 hours.

STRAPATSADA (SCRAMBLED EGGS WITH TOMATOES AND FETA CHEESE)

- *3 ripe tomatoes*
- *4 eggs*
- *1/2 tea cup olive oil*
- *fresh basil*
- *salt*
- *black pepper*
- *1/4 kilo feta cheese*
- *garlic (optional)*

Peel and grate the tomatoes.
Add them to the frying pan with
the oil. Heat for around ten minutes,
stirring lightly with a wooden spoon
until the liquid is absorbed. Add the salt,
pepper and crumbled feta cheese,
 stirring two or three times.
Delicious with fresh bread!

DOLMADAKIA

(STUFFED VINE LEAVES)

- *1/2 kilo vine leaves*
- *1/2 kilo rice (for soup)*
- *dill, finely chopped*
- *basil, finely chopped*
- *6 spring onions, finely chopped*
- *1 tea cup olive oil*
- *juice of 1 lemon*
- *salt and pepper*

Lightly steam the vine leaves
and strain. Place all the ingredients
in a bowl and mix well.
Add a spoon of the mixture
to each vine leaf and wrap carefully.
Lay the dolmadakia in a saucepan in
concentric circles. Add a little
hot water, just enough
to cover them.
Cover with a plate
and cook slowly
for around 1 hour.
Dolmadakia can
be eaten cold.

SANTORINI DOMADOKEFTEDES (TOMATO BALLS)

- *4 ripe tomatoes*
- *2 small onions • 2 cups flour*
- *olive oil • parsley • mint • basil • salt and black pepper*

Peel the tomatoes and chop into small pieces. Finely chop the onions and mix with the tomatoes. Add the mint, basil, parsley and pepper and mix all the ingredients together, gradually adding the flour until the mixture has softened. Shape the balls. Heat the olive oil in a frying pan, lower the heat and fry the tomato balls on both sides. Perfect with a glass of ouzo in Ano Meria, Santorini... in real life or in our dreams!

CRETAN DAKOS (BARLEY RUSK)

- *1 large barley rusk • 1 large ripe tomato • 1/2 tea cup spicy feta cheese, grated*
- *parsley, finely chopped • freshly ground black pepper • 3 soup spoons olive oil*
- *vinegar • oregano • a few olives*

Moisten the barley rusk and leave to dry. Drizzle with olive oil. Add the tomato, feta, oregano and parsley, and drizzle with the vinegar and oil. Garnish with black olives.

PEPPERS STUFFED WITH FETA CHEESE AND OLIVES

- *green peppers (long)*
- *feta cheese*
- *tomatoes*
- *parsley*
- *pure virgin olive oil*

Crumble the feta cheese in a bowl, gradually pour in the olive oil and mix well. Add the finely chopped tomato, parsley, salt, black pepper, and mix all the ingredients together with a little vinegar. Remove the top part and seeds from the peppers and stuff them with the mixture. Heat in an oven until the peppers are cooked.

ROAST PEPPERS

- *3 red peppers*
- *3 green peppers*
- *2 cloves garlic*
- *1/2 tea cup extra virgin olive oil*
- *a little vinegar*

Clean the peppers well, dry them and prick them at various points with a fork. Grill in an oven or barbecue over coal, until they start to blacken. Remove from the oven, rinse with cold water and peel. Arrange them on a serving dish and drizzle with olive oil and vinegar. Finely chop the garlic and sprinkle over the peppers.

"Ladera" dishes

(foods prepared in olive oil)

Olive oil is mentioned in recorded recipes from 2000 years ago. Ladera dishes, foods prepared in olive oil, are characteristic of Greek cuisine. They are eaten in summer and winter, accompanied by feta cheese, olives, fresh bread and salads. The proportion of olive oil used is fundamental to ensuring that the ladera dish is a success. They are cooked on a low heat in an open pan. Ladera dishes need good quality olive oil in order to be appetising and healthy. The olive oil is added to the food during the final stage of cooking.

POTATOES AND PEAS

- 1/2 kilo fresh or frozen peas
- 2 carrots, sliced
- 2 small onions, sliced thinly
- 2 potatoes, cubed
- 2 garlic cloves, crushed
- a bunch of parsley,
  finely chopped
- salt and black pepper
- 1 tea cup olive oil
- 3-4 tomatoes, skinned
  and finely chopped

Heat the oil and lightly fry the onion
and garlic. Add a cup of water, the peas,
tomatoes, potatoes, parsley, salt and pepper.
Cover the pan and leave to cook over a low heat
for one hour.

IMAM BAYALDI

- 6 long aubergines
- 4 onions
- 2-3 cloves garlic
- 3 tomatoes, finely chopped
- parsley • salt and pepper
- nutmeg
- 1 cup olive oil

Halve the aubergines lengthways and leave
in a colander with plenty of salt so that they
will strain and the bitter taste be removed.
Fry the onion and garlic in olive oil, add
the fresh tomatoes, finely chopped, salt
and pepper, parsley and nutmeg. Rinse
the aubergines in plenty of water, arrange
them in a baking tray and fill them with
the mixture. Cook in a medium over for
one hour.

OVEN-BAKED AUBERGINES WITH FETA CHEESE

- *2 large aubergines halved lengthways*
- *200 grams feta cheese*
- *3 large tomatoes chopped in a liquidiser*
- *2 soup spoons parsley, finely chopped*
- *1 clove garlic, finely chopped*
- *4 soup spoons extra virgin olive oil*
- *salt and black pepper*

Halve the aubergines lengthways and leave in a colander with plenty of salt for half an hour. Then rinse and dry them. Fry the aubergines, drain them and drizzle them with vinegar. Put them on a baking tray and cover with the tomatoes. Sprinkle over the garlic, parsley and crushed cheese. Pour the olive oil on top. Bake in the oven for 25 minutes.

OKRA

- *1 kilo okra*
- *1 cup virgin olive oil*
- *1 onion, finely chopped*
- *1/2 kilo tomatoes, finely chopped*
- *a little parsley*
- *salt and black pepper*

Clean the okra. Place them in a baking tray with salt and vinegar and leave out in the sun. Once they start to dry out, add the tomatoes, parsley, olive oil, salt, pepper and water so that the okra is just about covered. Cook in the oven for an hour.

BRIAM WITH POTATOES AND COURGETTES

- *1 kilo potatoes*
- *1 kilo medium courgettes*
- *1/2 kilo fresh tomatoes*
- *6 cloves garlic*
- *1 bunch parsley, finely chopped*
- *1 1/2 cups olive oil*
- *salt and pepper*

Clean, peel and slice the potatoes. Clean the courgettes and chop into thick, long and narrow slices. In a medium-sized baking tray arrange a layer of courgettes. Sprinkle with salt and pepper and half the parsley. Finely chop three cloves of garlic, peel and finely chop the tomatoes and pour half over the courgettes. Continue with a layer of potatoes, then another of courgettes and top off with the remaining potatoes, garlic, parsley and tomatoes and salt and pepper. Drizzle the food with olive oil. Add two to three cups of water and cook in the oven for around an hour. You can also substitute half the courgettes with aubergines.

ARTICHOKES

- *5 artichokes*
- *3 lemons*
- *4 spring onions, finely chopped*
- *3 potatoes*
- *3 carrots, sliced*
- *a little dill, finely chopped*
- *1 cup olive oil*

Clean and prepare the artichokes and rub them with lemon. Put the artichokes, potatoes, onions, carrots and dill in a large saucepan. Add the olive oil and cover with water. Heat for around 1 1/2 hours.

RUNNER BEANS AND POTATOES

- *1 kilo runner beans*
- *1 tea cup virgin olive oil*
- *2 carrots, sliced*
- *2 potatoes, chopped*
- *2 onions, thinly sliced*
- *2 cloves garlic*
- *parsley, finely chopped*
- *4-5 ripe tomatoes*
- *salt and black pepper*
- *sugar • cinnamon*

Heat the olive oil and fry the onions and
garlic until browned. Add the tomatoes,
peeled and finely chopped, the potatoes, carrots, parsley, salt
and pepper. Fry for five minutes. Add the beans and a cup of water.
Stir and cover the pan. Cook at a low heat for an hour.

ROAST POTATOES WITH ROSEMARY

- *1 kilo small round potatoes • 1 soup spoon rosemary • 2 cloves garlic*
- *8 soup spoons olive oil • 1 soup spoon mustard*
- *juice of one lemon • salt and black pepper*

Clean and salt the potatoes and arrange them in a baking tray.
Sprinkle with the rosemary. Add the garlic and drizzle with the oil.
Beat the mustard and the lemon juice together and drizzle over
the potatoes. Heat at 200 degrees for around half an hour.
To accompany barbecued meats.

ARTICHOKES WITH BROAD BEANS

- *1 kilo fresh broad beans* • *6 artichokes*
- *1 1/2 cups olive oil* • *5 fresh spring onions, sliced*
- *1 bunch dill, finely chopped*
- *2 lemons* • *salt and pepper*

Top and tail the beans. Remove the skin if it is tough. Wash the beans.
Clean the artichokes by removing the hard centres from the leaves and the stalk.
Chop the tips of the leaves and scrape the inner section to remove the whiskers.
Rub them with a lemon so as not to blacken and leave them in water. Fry the onions
in the olive oil until they are softened, along with the dill and the lemon. Complete
the sauce with 2 cups of water and add the beans and the artichokes. Add salt and leave
to bubble on a medium heat for around 1 1/2 hours.

STUFFED TOMATOES

- *8 large tomatoes*
- *For the filling:*
- *1 bunch parsley* • *8 small cups of brown and white rice*
- *salt* • *pepper* • *spices*
- *2 dessert spoons mint*
- *8 dessert spoons dry bread, crumbled*
- *potatoes, cubed (optional)*
- *the juice of 2-3 ripe tomatoes or tin tomatoes*
- *1 large onion* • *3 cloves garlic*
- *100 grams black currants*
- *100 grams pine cones*
- *1 aubergine*
- *1 cup olive oil*
- *2 soup spoons sugar*

Clean and dry the tomatoes. Open them at the bottom and remove the contents, chop contents in a blender. Leave in a casserole dish with the lid removed.

Filling: clean the aubergine and grate roughly. Sprinkle the aubergine with salt and leave to strain in a colander for 30 minutes. Chop the onions and the garlic, lightly fry in the olive oil until softened, add the aubergine flesh, tomatoes, salt and pepper and spices and cook slowly for 7-8 minutes. Then add the rice, parsley and mint, a little salt and a little sugar. Add a teaspoon of olive oil for each open tomato. Divide the filling between the tomatoes, sprinkle a little crumbled dried bread, pour over the tomato juice along with a little olive oil. Chop a few small potatoes into cubes and arrange them in between the tomatoes and heat in a medium oven for 40-50 minutes.

SNAIL STIFADO (STEW)

- *1 kilo large snails*
- *1 kilo spring onions*
- *1 1/2 cups olive oil*
- *7 cloves garlic*
- *1/2 cup vinegar*
- *1 dessert spoon rosemary*
- *3 bay leaves*
- *5 ripe tomatoes,*
  finely chopped
- *salt*
- *pepper*

Soak the snails over night in water, covering them with something heavy so they do not escape. Clean them well to remove all impurities.
Fill a saucepan with water, add the snails and heat over a flame. When the froth begins to rise to the surface (a little before coming to the boil) add the salt and stir roughly in one direction with a wooden spoon. This is a trick to remove the snails from their shells easier later. Leave to boil for 15 minutes then strain. With a sharp knife open a small hole in the back part of the shell. Rinse them in the water used to boil them to retain the flavour. Fry the spring onions and garlic in olive oil until browned. Add the tomatoes, bay leaves, rosemary, vinegar, salt and pepper and a little water. Cover and leave to boil.
When the onions are almost ready, add the snails. Leave the mixture to bubble for around 15-20 minutes until the sauce has thickened. Snail stifado is a wonderful mezze dish that can be found in many Greek tavernas. If the snails are collected from regions with much thyme and mastic trees this dish is even tastier.

Pulses

By pulses we mean beans, chickpeas, lentils, split peas, broad beans, peas, etc. These are considered to be one of man's basic foodstuffs. They contain proteins, carbohydrates and iron. The protein in pulses is equivalent to animal proteins. Pulses contain all the vital elements for the metabolism as well as many vitamins, especially vitamin B complex.

Pulses are prepared by being soaked in water overnight. The next day they should be strained and placed in a pan with fresh water and a little baking soda.

Cook over a low flame.

Add salt just before the cooking is completed, to prevent them from peeling and hardening. Olive oil is essential for cooking pulses as it softens them.

Pulses can be difficult to digest.

If you add a little mustard powder to the water whilst they are cooking this will prevent you from feeling bloated.

OVEN-BAKED GIANT BEANS

- 1 kilo "giant" beans
- 1 tin tomatoes or 4 ripe tomatoes, finely chopped
- 1 onion
- 2 cloves garlic
- parsley, finely chopped
- 1 cup olive oil
- salt and pepper

Soak the giant beans for 12 hours. Drain and boil slowly until they are softened.
Strain and put in a baking dish. Add the finely chopped onion, parsley, tomatoes, salt and pepper. Cover the tray with aluminium foil and heat in the oven at a medium temperature. If necessary, add a cup of warm water.

OVEN-BAKED SIFNOS CHICK PEAS

- 1/2 kilo chick peas
- 4-5 ripe tomatoes grated
- rosemary
- 1 onion, grated
- 1 cup olive oil
- salt and black pepper

Soak the chick peas for 12 hours so that they swell. Cook them without adding salt.
In a saucepan gently fry the onion in the olive oil. Add the tomatoes and cook for 15 minutes.
Put the chick peas in a clay dish, cover with the tomatoes, parsley, rosemary, salt and pepper and bake in the oven for half an hour.

BEAN SOUP

- 1/2 kilo of medium-sized haricot beans
- 4 medium size carrots
- 1 stick of celery
- 2 onions, finely sliced
- 1 1/2 cups of tomato juice
- 1 cups of oil
- salt
- pepper

Soak the beans in water overnight.
Then allow them to boil for 5 minutes
in the same water before pouring it away.
Put the beans in a saucepan along
with the carrots cut in thin rounds,
the celery (finely chopped) and the onion
and cover the ingredients with water.
Add the tomato juice, the oil, the salt
and the pepper. Allow to boil
until all the ingredients are tender.

CHICKPEA SOUP

- 1/2 kilo of chick peas
- 1 large onion,
  finely chopped
- 1 cup of oil
- 1 tablespoon baking soda
- salt
- pepper

Soak the beans overnight. Drain
them and put them in a large bowl
of water with the baking soda. Leave
for around an hour. Then rinse them
in plenty of water to remove the baking
soda. Put them in a casserole dish
with plenty of water. As soon as they
start to boil remove the forth from
the baking soda, then add the onion,
olive oil, slat and pepper and cook
until softened.

LENTILS

- *1/2 kilo lentils* • *1 carrot*
- *2-3 medium-sized onions, finely chopped*
- *2-3 cloves garlic*
- *1/2 cup olive oil*
- *around 6 cups water*
- *1 tablespoon vinegar*
- *2-3 tomatoes, finely chopped (optional)* • *salt* • *pepper*
- *1 teaspoon tomato paste*
- *2-3 bay leaves* • *oregano*

Soak the lentils overnight.
Put them in a casserole dish with plenty of water and bring to the boil 2-3 times, for around 5 minutes.
Remove the casserole dish from the flame and strain the lentils in a colander, discarding the water. Clean the casserole dish and add the lentils and remaining ingredients, except for the tomatoes. Leave to boil slowly. Around 15 minutes after they have been brought to boil add the tomatoes and olive oil. Once the lentils have cooked add the vinegar (optional).

PILIOS BEAN STEW

- *1 kilo dry beans*
- *2 cups finely chopped carrots*
- *celery, finely chopped*
- *2 spring onions, finely chopped*
- *4 ripe tomatoes, peeled and finely chopped*
- *100 grams bacon*
- *1 cup olive oil*
- *salt* • *black pepper* • *thyme*
- *1 small red pepper (optional)*

Soak the beans for 12 hours until they have softened. Drain, rinse and cook the beans in cold water. Add the carrots, onion, thyme, red pepper, pepper and tomatoes and heat for half an hour.
Fry the bacon and add to the beans a few minutes before cooking is completed along with the olive oil and salt.
Note: add olive oil to pulses just before cooking is completed so that it does not lose its vitamins. Accompany with olives, salted fish and feta cheese.

PIAZ BEANS

- *1/2 kilo small beans*
- *1 large onion, finely chopped*
- *parsley, finely chopped*
- *1/2 cup olive oil*
- *1 soup spoon vinegar*
- *capers*
- *oregano*
- *salt and pepper*
- *olives*

Soak the beans overnight.
Boil in a pan and drain.
Then put the beans
in a bowl with the onions,
parsley, oregano, capers
and seasoning
and mix well. Drizzle
with the olive oil and
the vinegar and garnish
with olives.

YELLOW PEA PUREE (FAVA)

- *1/2 kilo dried yellow beans (fava)*
- *1 large onion*
- *1 cup olive oil*
- *8 cups water*
- *oregano*
- *capers*
- *juice of 2 lemons*

Cook the yellow beans and the onion
in a pan with an open lid on a slow
flame, so that it does not swell.
Strain and put in a dish. Add
the olive oil and lemon juice and mix
well, until they have been absorbed.
Garnish with finely chopped onion,
oregano and capers.

Meat

Meat is of great nutritional value and is full of proteins. Meats are categorised as white meats (lamb, pork, chicken) and red meats (veal, beef, etc.). Meat contains phosphates, iron and many vitamins. It is essential for a healthy, functioning organism. It can be cooked in many ways and is best eaten when accompanied by raw or cooked vegetables.

LAMB WITH FRAGRANT SPICES

- *1 - 1 1/2 kilos lamb cut into individual portions*
- *5 cloves garlic*
- *4 leaves sage • rosemary*
- *1 tea cup white wine*
- *3 onions, finely chopped*
- *1/2 teacup olive oil*
- *salt • black pepper • lemon juice*

Pierce the meat at various points and insert the garlic. In a baking tray, sprinkle the chopped herbs and onion over the meat. Pour over the wine and olive oil and season. Cover with aluminium foil and cook in the oven for 1 1/2 hours. Remove the foil and cook for another ten minutes until browned. Serve with potatoes and dry red wine.

YIOUVETSI (BEEF STEW)

- *1 kilo beef chopped into portions • 1/2 kilo kritharaki (barley-shaped) pasta*
- *1 tin tomatoes or 5 ripe tomatoes, finely chopped • 1 cup olive oil*
- *salt and pepper*

Put the meat, olive oil, tomatoes, salt and pepper and a little water in a casserole dish and cook in the oven at a medium temperature. When the meat is almost cooked, add the kritharaki and stir well several times. Cook in a medium oven for a further half hour.

MINT KEFTEDAKIA (MEATBALLS)

- *1/2 kilo minced beef*
- *2 onions, grated*
- *2 slices bread, soaked in water and squeezed well*
- *2 cloves garlic, crushed*
- *parsley and mint, finely chopped*
- *1/2 tea cup olive oil*
- *salt • black pepper*
- *a little vinegar*

In a bowl, thoroughly mix the mince, bread, onion, garlic, parsley, mint, oil, salt and pepper. The more thorough the mixing, the softer the meatballs will be. Shape the meatballs, roll them lightly in flour and fry in olive oil. Serve immediately with fried potato chips and a Greek salad.

KOKINISTO (REDDENED) LAMB STEW

- *1 kilo beef chopped into portions*
- *2 onions, finely chopped*
- *1/2 cup olive oil*
- *1/2 kilo tomatoes, peeled and finely chopped*
- *1 teaspoon paprika*
- *1 clove garlic*
- *salt*

In a frying pan, heat the oil and brown the beef portions on both sides. Add the onions and stir lightly with a wooden spoon. Add the tomatoes, garlic and paprika and leave to bubble slowly for 1 hour on a low flame. Serve with rice or chips. This meal goes especially well during the winter.

CHICKEN IN RED WINE WITH FRIED POTATOES

- 1 chicken chopped into individual portions
- 1 clove garlic
- 2 cups red wine
- 1 bay leaf
- 1/2 cup olive oil

Flour both sides of the chicken and sauté in a large saucepan until browned. Pour over the wine and once the heat has subsided add the onion, garlic, bay leaf and 2 cups of water. Cover the pan and leave on a low heat for around an hour. Serve with fried potatoes.

COCKEREL AND MACARONI

- 1 cockerel, weighing around 2 kilos
- 2 onions, finely chopped
- 1 cup virgin olive oil
- 1 kilo ripe tomatoes or tin tomatoes
- salt and pepper
- 1/2 kilo macaroni

Clean the cockerel, dispose of the head, neck and feet and chop into portions.
In a casserole dish, heat the olive oil and sauté the onions.
Add the cockerel and brown on all sides.
Add the tomatoes. Cook slowly for around 2 hours.
Remove the cockerel from the casserole and add 6 cups of water.
As soon as it boils add the macaroni and cook for 5-6 minutes.
The macaroni absorbs the liquid and cooks in this way.
Serve with grated cheese.

CHICKEN WITH NOODLES

- *1 medium-sized chicken*
- *1/2 kilo of noodles*
- *4 ripe tomatoes*
- *2 onions, finely chopped*
- *1/2 cup of butter*
- *salt • pepper • cinnamon*

Clean and wash the chicken and put it into a pan with the onions to brown. When it has browned all over, add in the tomatoes, skinned and crushed in a vegetable blender. Sprinkle with cinnamon and add salt and pepper. Bring to the boil on a moderate heat adding 2 cups of water just before it reaches boiling point. Supplement the chicken stock with 2 more cups of water and when it starts to boil again, and the noodles. Allow to continue boiling on a low heat until all the moisture (or at least most of it) is absorbed. To prevent the noodles from sticking, the contents of the pan must be stirred frequently.

STIFADO (STEW)

- *1 kilo beef chopped into portions*
- *1 kilo spring onions*
- *3 cloves garlic*
- *1 cup olive oil*
- *1 tin tomatoes*
- *4 soup spoons vinegar*
- *2 bay leaves • 1 stick cinnamon*
- *salt and pepper*
- *1/2 cup water or beef stock*

In a casserole dish, heat the olive oil and sauté the beef. Add the onions and garlic and "extinguish" with the vinegar. Then add the tomatoes and remaining ingredients. Finally, add half a cup of warm water or stock. Cook over a low flame.

PASTICCIO

- *1 kilo of macaroni* • *1 kilo of mince* • *2 large onions, finely chopped*
- *2 cups of mashed tomatoes* • *1/2 cup of oil* • *1/2 cup of butter (for the macaroni)*
- *salt* • *pepper* • *10 cups of milk* • *1 cup of butter* • *1 cup of flour* • *8 eggs*
- *3 cups of grated cheese*

Put the mince and the onions in a large saucepan along with a little water and stir a couple of times, until the water has been absorbed. Add the olive oil and brown the mince, seasoning with salt and pepper. Add the tomatoes and allow the mixture to boil slowly. Boil the water in another large saucepan and cook the macaroni. Once they are cooked, strain and lay out half in a baking dish. Sprinkle with the grated cheese and put a layer of mince, of equal thickness, over the top. Lay out the remaining macaroni, sprinkle with cheese and pour over half a cup of olive oil. Prepare the bechamel sauce: heat one cup of olive oil in a pan and as soon as it begins to sizzle add the pepper and stir with a wooden spoon. Add the milk, stirring constantly so it does not become lumpy. It is better to heat the milk a little beforehand, to avoid the lumps. Then drop in the cheese (holding aside 2 tablespoons) and a little salt. Once the sauce has thickened remove from the flame. Beat the eggs well and add them slowly to the sauce. Pour the sauce over the tray and sprinkle with the remaining cheese.

YUVARALAK (MINCE AND RICE BALLS)
WITH EGG AND LEMON SAUCE

- *500 grams of mince*
- *1/2 cup of oil*
- *1/4 cup of rice* • *1 egg*
- *1 onion, medium-sized, finely chopped*
- *parsley, finely chopped* • *salt* • *pepper*
for the sauce: • *1 egg* • *2 lemons*

Mix the ingredients in a bowl and knead well. Mould into balls. Half fill a saucepan with water and melt the butter. Add some salt to the water and put the meatballs in one by one. When they are cooked, prepare the egg and lemon sauce according to the recipe for this sauce.

MOUSSAKA

- *2 kilos of large round aubergines • 1 kilo of mince • 1/2 cup of oil • 2 large onions*
- *5 ripe tomatoes • 1/2 cup of dry white wine • salt • pepper • grated kefalotiri cheese*
- *oil for frying • 2-3 portions of white sauce (bechamel)*

Peel, wash and cut the aubergines into large, thin slices. Salt and leave them to strain. Prepare the mince by browning it with the oil and onion, which should be finely chopped. Stop the browning process by pouring in the wine. Add the tomatoes, skinned and finely chopped, the salt and the pepper and allow to boil till all the moisture has been absorbed.
Pour the oil into a frying pan and fry the aubergines. Then spread them in a large roasting tin and sprinkle with grated cheese. After the first layer, spread the mince on top and then add another layer of fried aubergines. Then sprinkle again with the grated cheese and pour on the white sauce, so that the surface of the moussaka is covered with a thick layer of sauce. Finally, sprinkle some more cheese over this so that the surface becomes crisp.

Variations:

1. For easier serving and firmer portions, a layer of potatoes can be used.
These should have been cut into slices like the aubergines and fried in the same manner.

2. Moussaka with courgettes This is made by keeping the same quantities as above and using the same ingredients, but replacing the aubergines with courgettes cut into slices and fried, to be spread in the same manner in the roasting tin.

STUFFED COURGETTES

- *6 large courgettes • 1/2 kilo mince • 1 /2 cup of rice • 1/2 cup of oil*
- *2 medium-sized onions, finely chopped • parsley • salt and pepper*

Clean, scrape and wash the courgettes. Cut a small slice at one end and empty them by hollowing out with a spoon or special scooper. Knead the mince meat with the rice, the finely chopped onions, the parsley, also finely chopped, and the salt and pepper. Fill the courgettes with this mixture. Do not fill them up completely but leave enough room for the swelling of the rice. Put them in a saucepan and add water until they are almost covered, then add the olive oil. Use the resultant stock (juice) for the egg and lemon sauce and pour over.

SOUVLAKI AND PITTA BREAD

- *200 grams of lean meat (pork shoulder)*
- *2 pitta breads • 1 onion finely chopped*
- *1 firm tomato, sliced • parsley • salt*
- *red pepper • 1/4 cup of oil • oregano*

Dice the meat and sprinkle with salt, pepper and oregano. Divide the pieces of meat and put them on to the skewers. Put them to cook on the grill. Chop the onions and the parsley. Cut up the tomato into thin slices. Cook the pittas on the grill, coating them with oil. When the pieces of meat are tender, put them on to the pitta (one skewer for each pitta bread) and slowly draw out the skewer. Add the onion, the parsley, the tomato, sprinkle with red pepper and roll up the pitta.

SOUTZOUKAKIA (SPICY MEAT BALLS)

- *1/2 kilo of mince*
- *2 cloves of garlic, crushed*
- *1 teaspoon of cumin*
- *1 cup of soaked crustless bread*
- *salt • pepper*
- *1 cup of oil*
- *flour and oil for frying*

ingredients for the sauce:
- *1 cup skinned, mashed tomatoes*
- *2 cloves of garlic*
- *salt • pepper*
- *cinnamon • sugar • oil*

Mix the mince with the remaining ingredients and form into short, thick sausage shapes. Flour each soutsoukaki individually, fry and drain on kitchen paper.
For the sauce:
Heat a little olive oil in a large saucepan and fry the garlic for a couple of minutes until browned. Add the remaining sauce ingredients and bring to the boil.
Once the sauce stars to thicken add the fried soutsoukakia. Cook slowly, until the sauce has completely thickened.

STEWED VEAL WITH PEAS

- *1 kilo of lean veal or tender beef*
- *1 cup of butter*
- *1/2 cup of dry white wine*
- *1 teaspoonful of crushed thyme*
- *1/2 kilo of peas • 1/2 cup of oil*
- *salt • pepper*

Wash the meat and cut it into slices. Heat the butter well in a wide, shallow pan. Season the sliced pieces of meat and put them into the pan to brown. Pour in the wine as soon as it has browned and cover at once. Add the thyme and 2 cups of water and allow the meat to stew. Boil the peas in salted water. When they are almost ready, drain and add them to the meat. Allow to stew together for a while, then serve.

AUBERGINE SLIPPERS

- *6 aubergines • 1 onion • 1 cup of oil • 1/2   kilo of mince*
- *1 clove of garlic • salt • pepper • 2 ripe tomatoes*

Remove the stems of the aubergines and wash them well.
Cut them in half lengthwise and nick the insides. Coat them with oil, put them in a greased baking tin and allow to bake in the oven until quite soft. Put the oil in a pan and heat. Add the onion and allow to' soften, then add the mince, the salt, the pepper, the wine and the finely chopped parsley.
Allow this mixture to cook on a low heat for 30 minutes. Fill the aubergines with the mince mixture and cover with 1 tablespoon of the white sauce for each half aubergine.
Finally, sprinkle with the grated cheese and bake for 30 minutes in a moderate oven.

Fish
Seafood

Fish is one of man's most basic and necessary foods. It contains proteins of great nutritional value, phosphates, asbestos and vitamins.

Fatty fish are rich in vitamins A and D.

In general fish is far more easily digested than meat.

How to tell if a fish is fresh:

• The skin is solid and does not leave a depression if you press it with your finger • The eye is sharp looking with a red colour • It smells of the sea

How to prepare fish:

• Clean thoroughly • Remove the fins and whiskers

• De-scale using the edge of a sharp knife.

To remove the scales easily leave the fish in water with baking soda for 3-4 minutes • Remove the innards • Slice the stomach with a knife and remove the intestines • Clean well under a running tap

Fish can be cooked in many ways. Fish are fried using olive oil. Before frying them, sprinkle with lemon juice and vinegar and leave them for ten minutes. Then flour them (see the section on "Healthy Frying").

LOBSTER COOKED ON COAL

with lemon-flavoured oil and rosemary

Use cotton wool to block
all the holes in the lobster
(feet, tail, claws).
Clean thoroughly in cold water.
Fill a saucepan with salted
water and heat.
Once the water starts to
bubble add the lobster and heat
slowly for ten minutes.
Remove and leave to cool.
Halve the lobster lengthways
and heat over coal for around
ten minutes.
In a bowl, thoroughly mix
1 tea cup olive oil, 1/2 tea cup
lemon juice, rosemary, salt
and black pepper.
Pour this sauce over
the lobster.

LOBSTER AND MACARONI

- *1 lobster*
- *2 onions*
- *1/2 kilo no. 10 macaroni*
- *1 tin tomatoes*
- *1 cup olive oil*
- *salt and pepper • basil*

Put the lobster in a pan and add just enough water to cover it.
Boil slowly for 30 minutes. Remove the lobster and retain the water for the macaroni.
Remove the shell from the lobster and chop it into pieces. In a frying pan sauté the
onions, then add the tomatoes, basil and a little of the water from the lobster.
Leave to bubble slowly for 30 minutes. Add the lobster pieces and bring the mixture
to the boil. Boil the macaroni in the lobster water. Drain the macaroni, drop in
the lobster and sauce and mix well.

SAGANAKI SHRIMPS

- *1 kilo shrimps*
- *4-5 ripe tomatoes,*
  finely chopped
- *1/2 kilo feta cheese,*
  grated
- *1 soup cup*
  olive oil
- *salt*
- *black pepper*
- *parsley,*
  finely chopped

Heat the shrimps
with a little salt.
Clean, removing shells
and heads. Arrange in
a clay dish, add the oil,
tomatoes, salt, pepper
and parsley. Heat in the oven for 20 minutes.
Add the feta and heat for a further 10 minutes.

SHRIMPS WITH PILAFF

• 1 kilo of shrimps (or prawns) • 2 1/2 cups of rice • 1 cup of oil • 1 1/2 cups of tomato juice (or small tomatoes, skinned and crushed) • 1 onion, large and finely chopped • salt • pepper

Remove the whiskers from the shrimps
and wash well. Salt them and allow to
drain. Heat the oil and put in the finely
chopped onions. As soon as the onions
have softened, add the tomato juice,
the salt and the pepper.
Allow the sauce to boil for about
10-15 minutes. Then add 2-3 cups
of water and the rice. When the rice
is almost boiling, add the shrimps.
Allow to boil together for about
15 minutes until the water has been
absorbed and according to your
preference as to the softness
of the rice. To be served hot.

OVEN-BAKED WHITEBAIT

- *1 kilo whitebait*
- *4 fresh onions, finely chopped*
- *2 cloves garlic*
- *1 bay leaf*
- *1 cup olive oil*
- *3 tomatoes, sliced*
- *salt and black pepper*
- *parsley, finely chopped*

Clean the whitebait and rinse in plenty of cold water. Drain and put in a baking tray. Add the onions, garlic and parsley. Season and drizzle with oil and lemon juice. Cover with the tomato slices.
Heat in the oven for around 30 minutes.
Goes well with a glass of wine, especially if you can hear waves!

MARINATED WHITEBAIT

- *1/2 kilo very fresh whitebait*
- *2 cups extra virgin olive oil*
- *juice of 2 lemons*
- *salt and black pepper*

Clean the whitebait, slit them and remove the central bone. Marinade them in a bowl with the vinegar and a little salt for 12 hours. Rinse them and place in a bowl with the olive oil and a little crushed garlic, if desired. Garnish with lemon and finely chopped parsley.

FRIED SQUID

- *1 kilo small squid*
- *1 cup flour*
- *olive oil for frying*
- *salt*

Clean and prepare the squid.
Cut into slices, roll in the flour and fry on a high flame.

SPAGHETTI WITH MUSSELS

- *1/2 kilo spaghetti*
- *1 kilo mussels*
- *2 cloves garlic*
- *1 onion, finely chopped*
- *1 tin tomatoes, finely chopped*
- *parsley, finely chopped*
- *1/2 cup extra virgin olive oil*
- *salt • black pepper*

Clean the mussels and heat
in a saucepan on a high flame
without water until they open.
Remove them from their shells
and leave on a plate. In a frying pan,
heat the oil and lightly brown the garlic
and onion. Add the tomatoes, salt and pepper.
Lower the heat and cook the sauce slowly.
Add the mussels. In a pan boil some water and cook the spaghetti.
When done, drain and arrange on a serving dish. Cover with the mussel sauce.

FRIED COD WITH GARLIC DIP

- *1 kilo cod*
- *1 cup flour*
- *1 cup olive oil*
- *1 cup water*
- *yeast*
- *1 egg*

Chop the cod into pieces
and leave to soak for 12 hours.
Change the water 2-3 times to soak
the salt from the cod. In a bowl, mix
the water, flour, a little yeast and salt.
Mix well until a batter has formed.
Heat the olive oil in a frying pan,
dip the cod pieces into the batter
and fry. Serve immediately
with garlic dip.

SARDINES
IN VINE LEAVES

- *1/2 kilo large sardines*
- *olive oil*
- *vine leaves*
- *salt • black pepper*
- *oregano*
- *olive oil mixed with lemon juice*

Clean the sardines well and brush
with oil. Season.
Wrap them in the vine leaves.
Cook on a coal barbecue for around
ten minutes. Remove from the heat,
open and drizzle with oil and lemon
and oregano.

GRILLED SALMON

- *1 fillet salmon*
- *1 cup olive oil*
- *fresh basil, finely chopped*
- *fresh mint, finely chopped*
- *1 lemon*

Marinate the salmon in 1/2 cup
olive oil and the juice of half
a lemon. Leave for two hours.
Cook the salmon under a grill
or on a barbecue for ten minutes
on both sides. In a bowl, beat the
remaining olive oil and lemon juice
and pour over the salmon. Sprinkle
with the basil and mint.

OCTOPUS WITH OLIVE OIL AND VINEGAR

- *1 octopus or several small octopuses*
- *bay leaves • salt • vinegar • oregano*
- *1/2 cup olive oil*

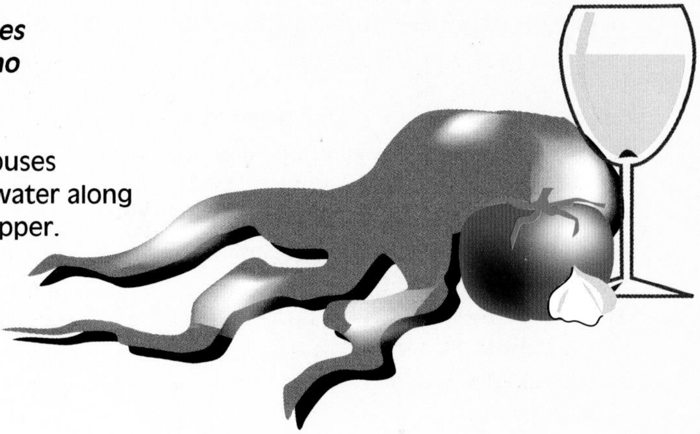

Clean one large or several small octopuses well and heat in a saucepan without water along with one bay leaf and a little black pepper. Heat at a low temperature until the octopus has softened. Slice into small pieces. Arrange on a serving plate and add olive oil, vinegar and oregano.Perfect in the summer with ouzo by the beach.

OCTOPUS WITH MACARONI

- *1 kilo octopus*
- *1 cup olive oil*
- *1 onion*
- *2 cloves garlic*
- *1 glass white wine*
- *3 ripe tomatoes, skinned or 1 tin tomatoes*
- *1/2 kilo short-cut macaroni*
- *salt • black pepper*
- *1 bay leaf*

Clean the octopus well and heat slowly in a pan without water until softened. Remove and chop into small pieces. In a large saucepan, heat the olive oil and fry the onion and garlic until browned. Add the wine and, once the steam has subsided, the finely chopped tomatoes, bay leaf, salt and pepper. Add a little water and when it begins to boil add the macaroni. As soon as the macaroni has cooked add the octopus and mix well. Serve immediately.

BOILED FISH WITH VEGETABLES

- *1 kilo fish* • *6 carrots*
- *8 medium-sized potatoes*
- *3 onions* • *2 tomatoes* • *celery*
- *1/2 cup of oil* • *salt* • *pepper*

Peel and wash the potatoes, the onions,
the carrots and the celery and put them in
a saucepan to boil whole with plenty of
water. Add the oil, the tomatoes. Remove the
scales, the innards and the gills of the fish.
When the vegetables are almost ready, add
the fish to them and allow to boil together.
Drain the fish and serve it in a oval dish,
garnishing it by placing the vegetables around
it attractively.

MARINATED FISH

- *1/2 kilo fish (gurnard, pike or sea bream)*
- *1 cup olive oil* • *juice of 2 lemons*
- *salt and black pepper* • *garlic, crushed*
- *1 cup water* • *flour* • *1 cup vinegar*
- *1 cup dry white wine* • *rosemary*

Clean the whitebait, open them
and remove the central bone.
Marinade them in a bowl with
the vinegar and a little salt for 12 hours.
Then rinse the whitebait and place
in a bowl with the olive oil and a little
crushed garlic, if desired.
Garnish with lemon and finely
chopped parsley.

OVEN-BAKED FISH WITH POTATOES

- *4 fish fillets*
- *1/2 kilo potatoes, sliced*
- *1 cup olive oil*
- *juice of a large lemon*
- *oregano*
- *salt • black pepper*

Clean the fish and place in a baking tray. Add the potatoes, oil, salt, pepper, oregano and lemon juice. Heat in the oven at 200° for half an hour.

FISH A LA SPETSIOTA

- *1 1/2 kilo fish*
  (bream, grouper, bass)
- *1 cup olive oil*
- *1/2 kilo onions, sliced*
- *1 1/2 cups tomato juice*
- *1 cup white wine*
- *1 cup dried breadcrumbs*
- *1/2 kilo tomatoes, sliced*
- *2-3 cloves garlic*
- *parsley, finely chopped*
- *salt • pepper • a little sugar*

Clean the fish, chop into slices, salt lightly and strain. Arrange the fish pieces in a baking tray and cover with the onion slices. Season and pour the white wine over all the pieces. Thoroughly mix together the olive oil, tomatoes, sugar, salt and pepper and pour half of this mixture over the fish. Combine the breadcrumbs, garlic and parsley and pour half of this over the fish. Then lay the tomato slices out over the fish. Pour over the remaining tomato and breadcrumb mixtures. Heat in a medium oven for 40-50 minutes.

Desserts

If you want the kind of figure seen in the pages of magazines, then desserts are not recommended! Even so, desserts are an ideal conclusion to a good meal and, for many, the most enjoyable way to treat our palettes. Delicate cookies with a coffee, tasty cakes and delicious baklavas, loukoumades, as well as "festival" cakes are hard to resist. Here we have chosen some recipes that you can prepare using good quality olive oil.

OILY KADAIF

- *1 kilo ready - made kadaif pastry*
- *1/2 kilo almond kernels*
- *1 1/2 tablespoons cinnamon*
- *1 tablespoon crushed rusk*
- *2 cups oil*

For the syrup:
- *1 1/2 kilos of sugar* • *4 glasses of water*
- *the juice of 1 lemon* • *vanilla*

Pound the almonds and mix with the cinnamon and the crushed rusk. Coat a baking tin with olive oil. Take one piece of the pastry and spread one tablespoonful of the mixture over it. Roll it up into a sausage roll shape and place in the baking tin. Continue in the same way with the rest of the pastry and when all of them are rolled up, put the oil on to heat. When it is hot, pour it over (1 full tablespoon) each roll.

Allow the rolls to bake in a moderate oven for 40 minutes until lightly browned. Allow to cool, then prepare the syrup. Boil the sugar with the water, add the vanilla and the juice of the lemon and then pour slowly over the rolls.

OLIVE OIL CAKE

- *1 1/2 cups olive oil*
- *1 1/2 cups orange juice*
- *1 1/2 cups sugar*
- *2 soup spoons cognac*
- *1 teaspoon ground cloves*
- *1/2 cup raisins*
- *1 packet self-raising flour*
- *1/2 cup olive oil*

Mix all the ingredients together
and blend in a blender.
Oil a baking tray with a little
olive oil and pour the mixture
into the tray. Bake for 40 minutes
in a medium oven.

OLIVE OIL COOKIES

- *2 1/4 tea cups olive oil*
- *1/2 kilo sugar*
- *1 cup cognac*
- *1 tea cup orange juice*
- *2 teaspoons soda*
- *2 teaspoons cinnamon
  powder*
- *1 teaspoon cloves,
  crushed*
- *peel from one orange*
- *2 kilos flour*
- *1/2 teaspoon salt*

In a large bowl mix all the
ingredients well until a soft
dough is formed.
Shape the cookies and cook
for half in an hour in a medium
pre-heated oven.

MELOMAKARONA (SMALL HONEY CAKES)

- *2 cups olive oil*
- *1 cup sugar*
- *1 cup orange juice*
- *1/2 cup cognac*
- *2 dessert spoons baking powder*
- *8 cups fine flour*
- *1 dessert spoon baking powder*
- *orange rind*
- *cinnamon*
- *ground walnuts*

For the syrup:
- *2 cups water*
- *2 cups honey*
- *2 cups sugar*

Stir the olive oil and the sugar together thoroughly and add the rest of the ingredients one-by-one (the baking soda diluted in the juice, the baking powder diluted in the juice).
Shape the mixture into small cakes and lay them out on an oiled baking tray. Heat in a medium pre-heated oven for 20-25 minutes.
When they are baked leave to cool. Prepare the syrup by mixing the sugar and the honey in the warm water. Arrange the melomakarona in a baking tray and drizzle them with the warm syrup. Sprinkle with ground walnuts.

TURNOVERS (DIPLES)

- *2 cups of flour*
- *3 eggs*
- *4 tablespoonfuls of brandy*
- *1 teaspoonful of baking powder*
- *2 tablespoonfuls of sugar*
- *olive oil*
- *1 cup of honey*
- *1/2 cup of warm water*
- *coarsely chopped walnuts*
- *cinnamon*

Mix the flour with the baking powder in a bowl. Make a well in the centre. Beat the eggs with the sugar and the brandy and add this to the flour, kneading well. Allow the dough to stand for half an hour and knead again. (Maybe half a cup of flour more may be required, but do not add this until you are sure if it is needed). Roll out the dough into a thin sheet then cut it into strips which can be tied in bows or knots or any shape you wish. Put plenty of oil in a frying pan to heat. The turnovers must be fried in very hot oil. When they have browned lightly, remove them from the heat and allow them to drain on absorbent kitchen paper.
Prepare the honey syrup by dissolving the honey in warm water.
Pour it over the turnovers, which have been placed on a flat dish.
Sprinkle with walnuts and cinnamon.

CRETAN XEROTIGANA (DRY FRIES)

- *3 teacups flour*
- *3 soup spoons orange juice*
- *4 soup spoons water*
- *3 soup spoons olive oil*
- *salt*

For the syrup:
- *1 teacup honey*
- *1 teacup sugar*
- *1 teacup water*
- *walnuts, roughly chopped*
- *sesame seeds*
- *cinnamon*

In a bowl, sift 2 1/2 cups of flour with salt. Open a hole in the middle and pour the orange juice, water and olive oil. Knead the pastry well until it is soft. Cover and leave to rise for half an hour. Roll the pastry into thin layers on a floured surface.

Slice the pastry using a toothed roller into strips 40 cm long and 2 cm wide. Take each strip and wrap it around your fingers, so as to create a roll about the size of a saucer.

In a frying pan heat enough olive oil to fry the xerotigana on a medium flame. Once the xerotigana have expanded remove them with a slotted spoon, before they start to go golden. Dip them in the syrup and sprinkle with walnuts, sesame seeds and cinnamon.

For the syrup:
Boil the sugar, honey and water for 3 minutes. Remove the froth.

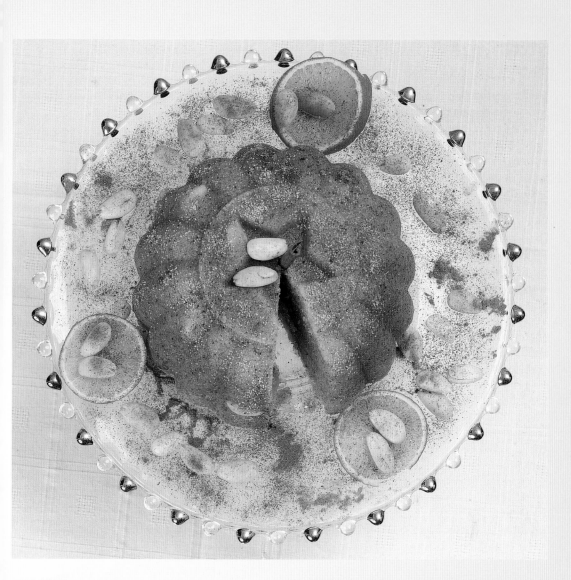

HALVA

- *2 cups coarse semolina*
- *1 cup olive oil*
- *2 1/2 cups sugar*
- *1/2 cup almonds*
- *5 cups water*
- *cinnamon*
- *3 cloves* • *lemon rind*

Heat the olive oil in a large saucepan and then slowly add the semolina, stirring constantly with a wooden spoon until it is golden. Add the almonds. Continue browning on a low flame, stirring constantly. Once the mixture has browned remove the pan from the flame and cover with a towel. Boil the water with the sugar for 2-3 minutes.
Add the syrup to the semolina mixture. Put the pan on a very low flame and cover with the lid for a few minutes until the syrup is absorbed. Sprinkle with the cinnamon.

HONEY PUFFS
(LOUKOUMADES)

- *650 grams flour*
- *1 full tablespoon yeast*
- *1 cup of lukewarm water*
- *1 tablespoon salt • oil for frying*
- *2 cups honey • 1 cup water*
- *cinnamon (optional)*

Put the flour in a bowl and mix it with the salt. Make a well in the centre and put in the yeast, having diluted it first in the lukewarm water. Combine the mixture, adding more lukewarm water to make a medium dough. Knead it for a little while then place the dough, covered with a clean cloth, in a warm place to rise. When it has done so (you can judge this by the small bubbles that will have formed on the surface), it is ready.

In a deep pan put plenty of oil to heat. Wet your hands and take a piece of the dough squeezing it in your fist to allow a small amount of the dough to be forced through the opening between your thumb and forefinger. Take a spoon and wet it, then scoop the dough from between your thumb and forefinger and place it in the boiling oil. When the puffs have browned slightly, remove from the oil and serve on a flat dish with honey and cinnamon poured over them.

BAKED DESSERT WITH OIL

- *1/2 cups olive oil*
- *1 1/2 cups orange juice*
- *1 1/2 cups sugar*
- *2-3 soup spoons cognac*
- *1 teaspoon baking soda*
- *1 teaspoon cinnamon*
- *1 teaspoon ground cloves*
- *1/2 cup walnuts*
- *1/2 cup raisins*
- *650 grams flour*
- *sesame seeds • olive oil*

In a bowl mix the olive oil, orange juice and sugar. Dilute the baking soda in the cognac and add to the bowl. Add the cinnamon and cloves and then add the flour a little at a time, stirring constantly. Then add the walnuts and the raisins. Oil a medium-sized baking tray and pour the mixture into it. Shake the tray until the mixture has spread out evenly. Sprinkle with the sesame seeds and bake for 40-50 minutes. Cut into squares.

YIANNINA BAKLAVA

- crushed walnuts
- 1/2 kilo fyllo pastry sheets
- 1 tea cup olive oil
- 2 slices dried bread, curmbled
- 1 cup sugar
- lemon peel
- cinnamon

For the syrup:
- 1 1/2 kilos sugar
- 4 cups water
- lemon juice

Lay half the fyllo pastry sheets on a baking tray, brushing each one with olive oil. Add the crushed walnuts, bread crumbs, lemon peel and cinnamon.
Cover with the remaining fyllo sheets, brushing each with olive oil. Mark out the individual pieces with a knife. Drizzle with a little olive oil. Cook in a medium oven for one hour. In a saucepan boil the water, sugar and lemon juice together for 5-10 minutes.
When the baklava has cooled down pour the hot syrup over it. Serve as soon as the syrup has been absorbed.

Cypriot
recipes

*I*n addition to being a beautiful
eastern Mediterranean island,
Cyprus is also a paradise
of gastronomic joys. The great variety
of tastes - many of which, as one
might expect, can also be encountered
in mainland Greece - make this island
not only an interesting destination
for travellers, but also for all those
who like their food.
We have selected some typical Cypriot
recipes for you, cooked of course with
plenty of select olive oil, Cyprus
also being an important olive oil
producing country.

AFELIA

- *1 kilo of pork chops with bone,*
- *2 cups dry dark red wine*
- *1/2 cup olive oil*
- *1 teaspoon salt*
- *1 teaspoon pepper*
- *2 tablespoons crushed coriander seeds*
- *warm water*

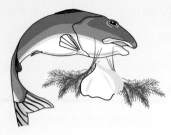

Cut the meat into strips four centimetres thick and marinate them in the wine in a glass basin. Cover well and refrigerate overnight. The next day drain the meat keeping one cup of the wine and sprinkle the meat with salt, pepper and coriander, and fry in olive oil till golden on all sides. Pour in the wine, heat up again and then add enough warm water to half cover the meat. Cover and simmer on low heat for an hour. This dish is served with pilaf, cracked wheat, small buttered potatoes, fresh lettuce, spring onions and radishes.

OVEN-BAKED FISH WITH SPICY GREEN VEGETABLE DRESSING

- *400-500 grams tope sliced into thin fillets*
- *salt*
- *self-raising flour*
- *lemon juice*
- *olive oil*

For the green dressing:
- *5 round spoons parsley,finely chopped*
- *2 1/2 spoons capers, drained and finely chopped*
- *2 fairly large garlic cloves, crushed*
- *3 1/2 spoons olive oil*
- *a little salt*
- *a little lemon juice*

If the fish fillets are long then slice them down the middle. Clean the fish well, salt, drizzle over the lemon juice and leave to stand for a few minutes. In the meantime, mix all the ingredients for the green mixture together in a bowl. Flour the fish well and heat the olive oil in a frying pan. Fry the fish on both sides. Serve the fish with the green dressing, without adding any more lemon as it is spicy enough.

HALLOUMI CHEESE PIES

- *1/2 cup olive oil*
- *1/2 cup melted butter*
- *4 cups flour*
- *1 tablespoon baking powder*
- *2 cups halloumi cheese,*
  coarsely chopped
- *1 cup boiling water*
- *1 teaspoon mint*
- *1 egg*
- *1/4 cup milk*
- *1/2 dessert spoon salt*

Put the chopped haloumi into a bowl
and pour over the boiling water.
Leave for 10 minutes until the cheese
has softened. Mix the flour, salt and
baking powder. Make a well in the centre
and pour in the butter with the olive oil,
mixing with our fingers. Drain the water
from the haloumi and add this liquid
to the dough. Knead well and leave to
stand for an hour. Roll out the dough
into a long, narrow sheet and lay the
cheese over it, cutting into 15 pieces.
Shape each piece into a ball with
our hands and press down into a pie
shape. Beat the egg with the milk
and spread over the surface of the
pies. Cook the haloumi cheese pies
in a medium oven for 45 minutes.

DAVAS
(SPICY BEEF OR LAMB)

- *800 grams beef or lamb with bones,*
  cut In small pieces
- *1 1/2 kilos large onions cut*
  into round slices.
- *800 grams ripe tomatoes peeled*
  and diced
- *3 cinnamon sticks*
- *1 1/2 tablespoons artysia**
- *1 1/2 tablespoons salt*
- *1 teaspoon freshly ground pepper*
- *3/4 cup vinegar*
- *1 cup olive oil*

Fry the small pieces of meat until it
reddens and then transfer to a ceramic
casserole. Fry the onions and when
they are soft add the vinegar. Then add
a little hot water with the seasonings,
the tomatoes and half the artysia.
Stir some more and empty into the pan
with the meat. Put the davas in the oven
and bake on low heat for 90 minutes,
stirring it from time to time.
Serve this typical Cypriot food hot,
sprinkled with the rest of the artysia
and accompanied by pilaff and a little
yogurt as a garnish on the plate.

*artysia = seasoning available in stores specialising
in Greek or Middle Eastern groceries.

KOUBEBIA WITH VINE LEAVES

- *around 40 large vine leaves*
- *600 grams mince*
- *1/2 glass rice, strained*
- *3-4 spoons olive oil*
- *black pepper and cinnamon*
- *a little dry basil*
- *parsley, finely chopped*
- *2 spoons lemon juice*
- *1 1/2 spoons tomato paste*
- *1 teaspoon roughly-chopped onion*
- *1 1/2 chicken stock cubes dissolved in 1/2 glass warm water*
- *1 glass ripe tomatoes, finely chopped*
- *5 spoons olive oil*

Drop the vine leaves into a little boiling water. Remove and strain. In a bowl, mix the mince, rice, black pepper, cinnamon, basil, parsley, onion, lemon juice, chicken stock, tomato paste and tomatoes. Spread out the vine leaves taking care that their shiny side is face down. Put about 2 teaspoons onto the edge of each leaf. Fold both sides in towards the centre and wrap into a roll, tightening lightly. Then place the koubebia into a large saucepan, add 4-5 spoons of olive oil and around 1/2 glass water and cover with a plate for pressure. Put the lid on and leave to cook on a low heat for around 40 minutes. It may be necessary to add more water.

BULGAR WHEAT

- *1/3 cup olive oil*
- *1 spring onion, finely chopped*
- *vermicelli (pilaff)*
- *2-3 red tomatoes chopped into small pieces*
- *2 1/2 cups warm water*
- *2 cups bulgar wheat*

Sauté the onion in olive oil, add the vermicelli until golden. Add the tomatoes and water and, when this has come to boil, the bulgar wheat and salt. Leave to cook until all the liquids have been soaked up.

MOUTZEDRA LENTILS

- *1 cup lentils*
- *4 cups water*
- *1 large onion, sliced*
- *1/2 cup olive oil*
- *a little salt*
- *4 cups water*

Clean and prepare the lentils.
Put them in a large saucepan with plenty
of water and bring to the boil, removing
the froth every so often. When they have
cooked add the rice, and more water
if this is necessary. In a frying pan,
sauté the onion in the olive oil and add
the lentils. Cook for a further five minutes,
adding salt just before the end.

SHEFTALIES

- *1 beef caul fat (stomach lining)*
- *1 kilo mince veal*
- *a little vinegar*
- *2 medium-sized onions,
  very finely chopped*
- *1 bunch parsley, very finely chopped*
- *1 dessert spoon black pepper*
- *1 dessert spoon cinnamon*
- *1 dessert spoon dry mint*
- *1/2 cup stale bread crumbs*
- *2 soup spoons olive oil*
- *salt*

Leave the caul fat for an hour in a bowl
of warm water, into which you have poured
the vinegar. Thoroughly mix all the
ingredients together. Use about 1 soup
spoon of the mixture for each sheftalia
and shape them into fat sausage-like
individual pieces. Wrap each shefalia
in the caul fat, cut into squares of around
10 x 15 cm. Cook the sheftalies arranged
next to each other on a grill with a medium
flame and cook on all sides.
Serve immediately.

POTATO SALAD WITH EGG

- *2 potatoes*
- *2 hard-boiled eggs*
- *1 spring onion, finely chopped*
- *1 spoon capers*
- *dry basil*
- *a little salt*
- *lemon juice or vinegar*
- *olive oil*

Clean the potatoes and boil
them in their skins. Once they
are cooked, remove the peel
and chop into small pieces.
Put them into salad bowl
and add the eggs chopped into slices,
onion, capers, mint and salt. Drizzle
with olive oil and lemon juice and mix well.

DOLMADAKIA WITH COURGETTE FLOWERS

- *20-30 courgette flowers*
- *1 cup rice*
- *salt and pepper*
- *parsley, finely chopped*
- *1 onion, finely chopped*
- *1 cup tomato juice*
- *half cup olive oil*
- *1 spoon lemon juice*

Clean and drain the rice. Heat the olive oil in a large saucepan. Fry the onion until golden. Lower the heat and add the rice and stir in well. Add the tomato and lemon juice and cook until all the liquids have been absorbed. Fill the courgette flowers with the mixture, folding their edges over towards the middle so that they form little squares to make the dolmadakia.
Arrange all the dolmadakia in a casserole dish and cover them with water. Cover with a plate for pressure and heat over a low flame until they are cooked.

FRIED LIVER

- *1 liver and offal*
- *1/2 cup olive oil*
- *3 onions, roughly chopped*

Clean the liver and chop into small pieces, separating the heart, lungs and black liver. Put it in a pan with a little water so it is just covered. Bring to the boil and then strain. Heat the olive oil in a frying pan. Fry the heart and lung pieces. Once they begin to cook, add the liver and roughly chopped onion.

OLIVE PIE

- *2 cups farina flour*
- *2 cups normal flour*
- *4 teaspoons baking powder*
- *1/4 cup black olives (de-seeded)*
- *1 cup chopped spring onions, with the leaves*
- *1 cup fresh coriander*
- *2 teaspoons dry mint*
- *1 cup olive oil*
- *1 cup orange juice*
- *sesame seeds*

In a large bowl add all the flour, baking powder, olives, onions, coriander, mint, olive oil and most of the orange juice and knead together well. Lay the mixture out in a glass baking dish, pour the remaining orange juice over the whole of the surface and sprinkle with the sesame seeds. Cook the olive pie in a preheated oven for around 50-60 minutes.

CYPRIOT DACHTYLA (FINGERS)

- *3 cups flour*
- *1/2 teaspoon salt*
- *1/3 cup olive oil*
- *1 egg yoke*

for the filling:
- *1 1/4 cup coarsely ground almonds*
- *3 tablespoons sugar*
- *1/2 teaspoon cinnamon*
- *1 egg white*

for the syrup:
- *1 cup sugar*
- *1/2 cup honey*
- *3 cups water*
- *1 rind of a large lemon*
- *1 cinnamon stick*
- *3 teaspoons lemon juice*

for frying:
- *3 cups olive oil*

for sprinkling:
- *1/2 cup finely chopped almonds*
- *1/3 cup sugar*
- *1/2 teaspoon powdered cinnamon*

Mix the flour and the salt and make a small hole in the centre.
Pour the oil into it and gently mix it with the fingertips. Add the water and the egg yoke while continuing to knead.

When the dough is soft, shape into balls and leave for one hour.
Prepare the filling. Beat the egg white with the sugar and add the almonds and the cinnamon.
Then prepare the syrup:
first boil the lemon peel and cinnamon in water for 5-6 minutes and leave it in the saucepan. Add the sugar and honey to the hot water and simmer over a low flame for 5 minutes. Then remove from the flame and add lemon juice.
Return to the dough, knead it a little longer and then form it into little balls.
Roll these balls one by one into rectangular pieces 11 x 9 cm and a sheet 1/4 cm thick. At the narrow edge of each sheet put a teaspoon of the filling and then roll up.
Press the ends together with a fork to seal and set each completed "finger" on a floured surface.
Fry in hot oil until golden (about 2 minutes on each side).
Lift and drain with a slotted spoon and put them immediately into the cold syrup. Take them out of the syrup after two minutes, drain again and sprinkle them with the mixture of almonds, sugar and cinnamon.

CYPRIOT CHEESE & RAISIN PASTRIES (FLAOUNES)

- 2 teaspoons brewer's yeast
- 1/2 cup warm water
- 1/2 cup warm milk
- 1 teaspoon chopped machlepi*
- 1 teaspoon chopped mastic
- 2 teaspoons sugar
- 7 cups flour
- 1 teaspoon salt
- 4 eggs lightly beaten
- 1/4 cup olive oil

ingredients for the filling:
- 1/4 cup melted butter
- 1 teaspoon mastic
- 1 teaspoon sugar
- 1 teaspoon baking powder
- 1 tablespoon flour
- 5 cups grated kefalotyrl (even better if Cypriot talariou cheese Is used)
- 3 cups Cypriot halloum cheese grated
- 4 tablespoons fresh mint finely chopped
- 1 cup sultana raisins • 5 beaten eggs

for basting:
- 2-3well-beaten eggs
- 1/3 cup unroasted sesame seeds

Dissolve the yeast in a small bowl with warm water and add warm milk.
Grind the machlepi, mastic, and sugar in a mortar, then mix together in a bowl.
Poking a small hole in the centre, mix the butter and oil together, and pour in.
Blend the mixture with your fingers while adding the milk and the eggs.
Transfer the dough to a floured marble surface and knead till it becomes springy
(for 5'-10') then make a ball of it. Put in a warm bowl and cover with oiled baking paper,
then place a towel on top and leave it rise for two hours in a warm place.
During that time prepare the filling. Grind the mastic and mix it with the baking
powder. Stir the grated cheese, flour and all the rest in a large bowl, add the mint
and then the raisins and the eggs. After mixing, cover and leave in a warm place.
Prepare the oven at a moderate temperature. Take the risen dough, knead
it a little more and fashion it into balls. With a rolling-pin roll each ball into a sheet
1/4 cm thick and cut out circles 15 cm in diameter, wetting the edges slightly
with water. Put two tablespoons of the filling in the centre and fold two sides
of the circle toward each other and then the top and bottom of the circle, until
the filling is half-covered. Press the four corners together with a fork to join them.
When all the flaounes are ready baste them with beaten egg and sprinkle
with the sesame seeds.
Bake for 40 minutes until golden.

* These flavourings can be found at Greek or Middle Eastern markets.

MYZITHRA CHEESE BUREK (PATTIES)

- *3 cups of flour*
- *1/2 teaspoon salt*
- *1/3 cup of olive oil*
- *1 egg yolk*
- *1 cup water • oil for frying*
- *powdered sugar*

for the filling;
- *2 cups unsalted myzithra cheese*
- *1/2 cup salt*
- *1 egg white*
- *1 desert spoon ground cinnamon*
- *2 table-spoons milk*

Mix the flour with the salt and sift onto a suitable surface. Open a well in the centre and pour in the olive oil, mixing with the tips of our fingers. Slowly add the egg yolk and the water, working the pastry constantly until it is soft.

Leave for an hour and prepare the filling. Melt the myzithra thoroughly and mix in the sugar and cinnamon. Beat the egg white with the milk and mix into the myzithra mixture. Return to the pastry, kneading it a little further. Make 3-4 balls and roll each ball out into a thin layer of pastry. With the aid of a glass, cut out little piea with diameters of 10 cm. Put a spoonful of the filling in the centre of each pie and fold over, sealing with the aid of a fork.

Arrange in a floured tray. Fry in hot oil until browned.

These Cypriot burek are served on a hot dish, sprinkled with powdered sugar.

Healthy frying

Olive oil contains a high degree of oleic acid
and so even when it is fried it does not undergo changes
that are bad for our health. The foods that are fried in olive oil
form a thin and attractive protective crust
and so do not absorb the oil, in contrast to other fats
which penetrate to the interior.
Because olive oil has a high liquid content, which is gradually
released during frying, the temperature of the oil
does not exceed 100-150 degrees.

Basic principals for correct frying

• Fry with a good quality frying pan.

•We do not need to use extra virgin olive oil,
an ordinary virgin olive oil will do.

• Heat the olive oil on a low flame
and then slowly increase the heat.

• The olive oil must cover
the food that is being fried.

• Do not add more oil during frying.

• Remove the food that is being fried,
add more olive oil, heat it
then continue frying.

• Remove the food carefully
from the frying pan and be careful
not to splatter the oil.

• The same olive oil can be used
up to five times.

Measuring instruments

The ordinary medium-sized teacup is the basic unit of measurement in the recipes in this book. The table which follows provides some conversions to help those who prefer to use other systems of measurement.

- **1 cup of flour** equals **16 (dessert) spoonfuls or 120 grams.**
- **1 cup of milk** equals **16 spoonfuls or 225 grams.**
- **1 cup of sugar** equals **16 spoonfuls or 225 grams.**
- **1 cup of olive oil** equals **16 spoonfuls or 240 grams.**
- **1 cup of honey** equals **16 spoonfuls or 350 grams.**
- **1 cup of water** equals **16 spoonfuls or 240 grams.**
- **1 cup of rice** equals **225 grams.**
- **1 cup of semolina** equals **175 grams.**
- **1 cup of grated cheese** equals **110 grams.**
- **1 cup of cream** equals **225 grams.**
- **1 soupspoon of liquid equals 3 dessert spoons.**
- **1/4 of a cup of liquid equals 4 dessert spoons.**

- **1 cup of spring onions** requires **8 onions.**
- **1 cup of onions, finely chopped,** requires **1 large onion.**
- **1/2 cup of onions, finely chopped,** requires **1 medium-sized onion.**

Oven temperatures

- 250° F or 120° C ....**very slow**
- 300° F or 150° C ....**slow**
- 350° F or 177° C ....**medium**
- 375° F or 180° C ....**medium-hot**
- 400° F or 205° C ....**hot**
- 450° F or 232° C ....**very hot**

Index of recipes

Text: KATERINA TSOUCHTIDI
The recipes: «Olive oil cake», «Oily kadaif», «Cretan xerotigana», «Baked dessert with oil»,
«Loukoumades», «Afelia», «Haloumi cheese pies», «Davas», «Koubebia with vine leaves», «Sheftalies»,
«Cypriot fingers», «Cheese and raisin pastries (flaounes)», «Patties with myzithra cheese», «Greek salad»,
«Cauliflower salad», «Beetroot salad», «Garlic sauce», «Briam with potatoes and courgettes»,
«Artichokes and broad beans», «Snail stifado», «Bean soup», «Chickpea soup»,
«Kokinisto lamb stew», «Chicken and hilopita pasta», «Pasticcio», «Moussaka»,
«Yuvarlak (meat balls with rice)», «Casserole beef and peas», «Shrimps and pilaff»,
«Boiled fish and vegetables», «Marinated fish», «Fish ala spetsiota»,
are taken from the book written by Sofia Souli, *Gastronomy - Greek Cookery and Wines,*
M. TOUBIS EDITIONS S.A.
Presentation of recipes: XENI KANELLOPOULOU
Art editing: M. TOUBIS S.A. - N. PETROVAS (recipes)
Photographs: HELLENIC IMAGE BANK

Production - Printing: M. TOUBIS S.A.

General index